ALEX KATZ

RICHARD MARSHALL

ALEX KATZ

WITH AN ESSAY BY

ROBERT ROSENBLUM

WHITNEY MUSEUM OF AMERICAN ART
IN ASSOCIATION WITH

RIZZOLI INTERNATIONAL PUBLICATIONS, INC.

THIS EXHIBITION IS SUPPORTED IN PART BY A GRANT FROM THE AMERICAN CAN COMPANY FOUNDATION

Marshall, Richard.
   Alex Katz.
   "Dates of the exhibition, March 13–June 15, 1986"—T.p. verso.
   Bibliography: p.
   1. Katz, Alex, 1927–   —Exhibitions. I. Katz, Alex, 1927–   . II. Rosenblum, Robert.   III. Whitney Museum of American Art.
N6537.K32A4   1986   759.13   85-31460
ISBN 0-87427-048-0
ISBN 0-8478-0717-7 (Rizzoli International)
Copyright © 1986

Cover: *Blue Umbrella # 2*, 1972.

WHITNEY MUSEUM OF AMERICAN ART
945 MADISON AVENUE
NEW YORK, NEW YORK 10021

ACKNOWLEDGMENTS

It has become increasingly apparent that Alex Katz is one of the most important American artists to have emerged since 1950. Throughout his career, which has now spanned more than thirty years, Katz has produced a remarkable and impressive body of work that constitutes an original and unique aspect of modern realism. This publication and the exhibition that it accompanies present over ninety paintings, cutouts, and collages in a survey of Katz's career since 1951. It is the largest presentation of Katz's work to date and has been realized through the efforts of many people. I would like to extend sincere thanks to the artist for his continued cooperation and enthusiasm during the preparation of the exhibition and publication; and deep appreciation to Ada Katz, the artist's most frequent, familiar, and profound subject, for her invaluable presence and important contributions to the project. I am grateful to Tom Armstrong, Director of the Whitney Museum of American Art, for his interest in and support of the exhibition, and to the entire staff of the Museum for their continued efforts in the realization of the exhibition and book. Especially appreciated is the assistance of Deborah Felstehausen in coordinating the research, loan, and photograph requests; and the help of Maureen Campbell, Sue Felleman, Frasher Hudson, and David Lurie in assembling biographical and bibliographical material. Alex Katz's gallery representatives—Pierre Levai at Marlborough Gallery Inc., New York, and Robert Miller and John E. Cheim at Robert Miller Gallery, New York—provided valuable assistance and consideration. In addition, I would like to acknowledge the generosity of the owners who have lent works to the exhibition, especially Paul J. Schupf for lending a number of paintings from his outstanding and extensive collection of Alex Katz's works.

RICHARD MARSHALL
ASSOCIATE CURATOR, EXHIBITIONS

CONTENTS

FOREWORD

Gertrude Vanderbilt Whitney established the collection and programs of the Whitney Museum of American Art with a dedication to realism. Her friends and advisers were artists trained in the realist tradition formed in the late nineteenth century by Thomas Eakins at the Pennsylvania Academy of the Fine Arts and continued in the twentieth century at the Art Students League in New York. Mrs. Whitney believed that The Eight and their successors, such as Edward Hopper and Reginald Marsh, as well as the Social Realists working during the 1930s, were among the truly significant artistic contributors to an understanding of Americans and American life.

In the years following World War II, the realist tradition in American art was generally eclipsed—first by the achievements of the Abstract Expressionists, then by those of the Minimalists. Despite these prevailing aesthetics, Alex Katz chose to work in a representational manner. Through his focus on both formal and stylistic elements of portraiture as interpretations of our society, he has created a singularly personal idiom that is expressively American. This exhibition, organized with great care by Richard Marshall, Associate Curator, surveys the evolution of Katz's approach to realism and portraiture, and his depictions of contemporary life, particularly in New York City. The ability of this artist to present a broad range of aesthetic and intellectual concerns within the framework of realism is unmatched.

The Whitney Museum has had a long association with the artist, exhibiting his work in numerous group exhibitions since 1960, and organizing a major traveling exhibition of his prints in 1974. In 1964, the Whitney Museum was the first museum to acquire a Katz painting, *Eli* (1963), for its collection (the first of four important Katz paintings to enter the Museum's Permanent Collection). I have known Alex Katz for over fifteen years and have continued to admire and respect his ability to synthesize the realist and abstract traditions in American art.

We are indebted to the artist for his cooperation and his respect for our efforts, and to the owners of his paintings, collages, and cutouts who have graciously joined us in this endeavor. I am pleased that the Whitney Museum, an institution that was built upon respect for American realism, is presenting his important talents to a larger public.

TOM ARMSTRONG
DIRECTOR

ALEX KATZ: SOURCES OF STYLE

RICHARD MARSHALL

Style and appearance are the things I'm more concerned about than what something means. I'd like to have style take the place of content, or the style be the content. . . . I prefer it to be emptied of meaning, emptied of content. [1]

Alex Katz is a complex figure to unravel. His works reveal conflicting and opposing impulses and elicit contrary responses. They are often called slick, stylish, and unrealistic likenesses of their subjects. They are, but not in a pejorative sense. They are technically and assuredly rendered with smooth, confident application of oil paint. They are glossy, bright, optimistic, direct, aggressive, and well composed, as is all of the best American visual art. But Katz's works can be at the same time passive, moody, ambiguous, and awkward. Characteristically, they display a shallow visual space that acknowledges the two-dimensionality of a painting and the tendency toward a reductive attitude in presentation; but they still elicit a deep resonance of psychological innuendo. Although portraiture is Katz's chosen mode of expression, allegiance to authentic physical features and personality evaluation is not his goal. Katz's Adas, Vincents, couples, and bathers are contemporary symbols. Their generalized countenances serve as vehicles for the exploration of the formal aspects of picture-making, while allowing for multiple readings that hint at narrative. Katz's astonishing achievement is to have reconciled abstraction and realism in post–World War II America.

Fig. 1
Edouard Manet, *WOMAN WITH A PARROT*, 1866
Oil on canvas, 72⅞ × 50⅝ (185.1 × 128.6)
The Metropolitan Museum of Art, New York; gift of
Erwin Davis, 1889

Fig. 2
Pablo Picasso, *LES DEMOISELLES D'AVIGNON*, 1907
Oil on canvas, 96 × 92 (243.8 × 233.7)
The Museum of Modern Art, New York; acquired
through The Lillie P. Bliss Bequest

Katz accomplished this feat by choosing from the visual, literary, and social stimuli surrounding him those attitudes and features that best suited his aesthetic stance. Painting representationally was never in question: "I knew I had to go with what I saw, the objective world, and that was what I was going to paint and that was all there was to it."[2] The real question for Katz was how to make a representational painting as modern, sophisticated, and grand as the Abstract Expressionist painting he admired. He wanted to create a painting that would compete with the philosophy and energy of a Kline or a de Kooning. Because Katz was well versed in the history of art, earlier figures also gained new importance for him. He acknowledges Pollock as the artist who opened up these vistas for him: "When I saw Pollock, I realized he had sensation, energy and light, and it seemed much more like the motif I was painting than my paintings. . . . The paradox with Pollock is that as he questioned the 20th-century French painting he made me reconsider other European artists: Tintoretto, Fragonard, Velásquez and Watteau. . . . Pollock made it possible for me to participate. The establishment of sensation painting was something I could relate to my experience. . . . The establishment of a grand impersonal style offered many possibilities for a large number of artists."[3]

Katz's reevaluation of modern European masters also clarified his attraction to what he refers to as "high style" art.[4] He defines this as a type of painting that is ambitious, large-scale, elegant, reflective of a specific time period, yet impersonal and timeless; art that displays "self-indulgence in a big art form, rather than self-indulgence in personal feelings."[5] High-style painting is typified for Katz by Manet, Matisse, Picasso, and Léger, among others, and in the work of each he observed affinities to his own attitudes that provided inspiration and afforded him the freedom to pursue his own approach to realism.

Ada in Blue Housecoat, 1959 (Pl. 36) is Katz's *Woman with a Parrot* (Fig. 1). He saw in Manet a painter of contemporary urban life whose works made reference to earlier art but were very modern in their attention to light and color over subject matter. Manet's non-sentimental portraits, with their large flat planes of color, served as an example to Katz of specific yet generalized portraiture. A recent description noted that Manet's "work offers the most varied images of contemporary life, with the grandeur of classical painting and the freedom of modern art; and it is in this duality that his individuality lies."[6] This observation is an equally appropriate description of Alex Katz's position in recent art history.

Fig. 3
Henri Matisse, *DANCE*, 1909
Oil on canvas, 102½ × 153½ (260.4 × 389.9)
The Museum of Modern Art, New York; gift of
Nelson Rockefeller in honor of Alfred Barr, Jr.

Fig. 4
Fernand Léger, *THREE WOMEN*, 1921
Oil on canvas, 72¼ × 99 (183.5 × 251.5)
The Museum of Modern Art, New York; Mrs. Simon
Guggenheim Fund

Picasso offered Katz another source of ideas about representation, figuration, and abstraction. *Les Demoiselles d' Avignon* (Fig. 2) is a monumental composition that crowds five figures into an ambiguous and shallow space. The outlining of figures and the flat planes of color defining a skewed perspective had obvious appeal, but what spoke most forcefully to Katz was the fact that Picasso planned the composition of the painting. For Katz, a painting is conceived through sketches and an outlined cartoon on canvas rather than, as in Abstract Expressionism, "found" in the act of painting. Katz's multiple-portrait paintings, such as the early *The Black Dress*, 1960 (Pl. 40), suggest a similar type of carefully pondered figure placement. His composition of six Adas required deliberate planning in order to build a powerful and legible grouping of figures. Ada is also seen full face and in profile, a conceit that may represent a parsing of Picasso's device of simultaneous views in a single face. *Place*, 1977 (Pl. 78), a later multiple portrait of five different people, recalls as well Picasso's rejection of traditional Renaissance space; as Roberta Smith describes *Place*, it "is one of Katz's most powerfully primitive and abstract images. . . . This forceful, stacked-up, top-heavy composition doesn't bother explaining how all the heads and shoulders physically fit into the

shallow space, much less where the rest of their bodies might be."[7]

Katz likes to take those kinds of liberties. He will forsake realism for the compositional success of a picture, a freedom he attributes to the influence of Matisse: "A lot of great representational art is not involved with being realistic at all. . . . Matisse is my hero for realistic painting. People think realism is details. But realism has to do with an over-all light, and having every surface appear distinctive."[8] Matisse's *Dance* (Fig. 3) was particularly important for Katz's early development. *After Softball*, 1953, and *Two Figures*, 1954 (Pls. 3, 5), display a Matisse-inspired flatness, implied motion, and broad, flat color areas defining abstracted shapes that become trees, road, or figures. Katz's *Ada in White Dress*, 1958 (Pl. 29), a later, more confident and powerful work, beautifully employs a Matisse-like color application of vibrant, sharp green around a schematically outlined, lonesome, and unmodulated figure. As Matisse used descriptive color in *Dance*, Katz has laid down a flat, over-all surface that releases the full strength of the color and fuses the image and ground together. Léger (Fig. 4) also offered Katz a related aspect of figuration—unromantic, mundane, and conventional subject matter, which appealed to Katz because it deemphasized con-

Fig. 5
Arshile Gorky, *THE ARTIST AND HIS MOTHER*, 1926–29
Oil on canvas, 60 × 50 (152.4 × 127)
Whitney Museum of American Art, New York; gift of
Julian Levy for Maro and Natasha Gorky in memory
of their father 50.17

Fig. 6
Willem de Kooning, *QUEEN OF HEARTS*, 1943
Oil and charcoal on board, 46⅛ × 27⅝ (117.2 × 70.2)
Hirshhorn Museum and Sculpture Garden, Smithsonian
Institution, Washington, D.C.

tent, allowing attention to be directed to structure, composition, color, and style.

> *The representational painting in America, post–World War II, developed. . . . mostly out of abstract painting: Willem de Kooning and Hans Hofmann being the main influences. . . . I developed an attitude that a painting could deal with specific information about the external world and that it, in itself, could be the subject matter rather than a social or philosophic illustration. . . . representational painters in the United States, in the 1950s, kept the social and philosophical content minimized, with the emphasis placed on formal values.* [9]

Among Katz's earliest works are a series of landscapes that explore formal attributes of painting. Like *Winter Scene*, 1951–52 (Pl. 1), they were painted outdoors, following the two summers he spent at the Skowhegan School in Maine, where he came to appreciate painting directly from nature. These paintings were also translations of the quickness of Kline (Fig. 8) and the light Katz saw in Pollock's drip paintings: "Pollock dominated my vision, but I could see the landscape—subject matter —through his abstract work." [10] *Winter Scene* makes literal the representational suggestion that Pollock later made more apparent in *Blue Poles* (Fig. 7). Katz's work is an abstracted representation of the impression of light

coming through a stand of trees, executed in quick, fluid brushstrokes that expand beyond the edges of the canvas. His attention to light is evident in his earliest works and it never ceases, even in the portraits that he began soon after these landscapes: "I got more specific because I got tired of all-over painting. . . . I had to modify my approach and work more indirectly over a longer period of time. I'm still involved with light—an absolute present-tense light—but it can't be achieved spontaneously. It has to be reconstructed." [11]

Throughout his career Katz has addressed more fully the issue of specific types of light, and his titles frequently make clear his intention of depicting the light associated with various times of day—*Swamp Maple, 4:30*, 1968, *Twilight*, 1975, *Night*, 1976 (Pls. 54, 74, 75); and times of year—*October #2*, 1962, *December*, 1979 (Pls. 42, 82). Other works, although less specifically titled, deal with the impression of bright sun—*Ada with Superb Lily*, 1967, *Vincent with Radio*, 1974, *Roof Garden*, 1975 (Pls. 53, 68, 71); light reflected off water—*Blue Umbrella #2*, 1972, *Swimmer #3*, 1973, *Eleuthera*, 1984 (Pls. 66, 69, 94); and artificial interior light—*The Cocktail Party*, 1965, *Thursday Night #2*, 1974 (Pls. 49, 76).

Katz's rejection of the all-over gestural approach was a result of his perception that Abstract Expressionist art, especially that of his contemporaries among the second-

Fig. 7
Jackson Pollock, *BLUE POLES*, 1953
Oil on canvas, 83 × 192½ (210.8 × 489)
Australian National Gallery, Canberra

generation New York School painters, had become mannered. Katz had selectively appropriated the philosophical and formal attributes of Abstract Expressionist work, but he was committed to the representational approach and determined to clarify, refine, and define his own attitude about realism. Frank O'Hara observed that at this time in his development, "Katz was pulling together his enthusiasms and influences into a congruent assemblage. . . . He freed his own painterly feelings and widened their range of possibility precisely at the moment when he was focusing them on a specific intention. . . . Katz has found a liaison between the personal and the general, the intriguing dialogue without which one is left with either formalism or expressionism."[12]

The early portraits—*Track Jacket*, 1956, *Ada in Black Sweater*, 1957, and *Self-Portrait (Cigarette)*, 1957 (Pls. 7, 26, 27)—exhibit the rawness of a gestural realist approach but display a tightening up of composition and restriction of color. Here Katz has eliminated any background detail or reference and centered a roughly outlined figure cropped at the waist or knees. These works mark the beginning of his full concentration on portraiture, and coincide with his marriage to and ongoing fascination with Ada. And it was a kind of portraiture—expressive in gesture, yet generalized in details—with

precedents in American figurative works by Gorky (Fig. 5) and de Kooning (Fig. 6), both artists whose works became increasingly abstract while retaining representational allusions.

In 1958–59, Katz produced an important group of pictures that resolved and surpassed issues explored in earlier paintings. These works, such as *Irving and Lucy*, 1958, *Bather*, 1959, and *Paul Taylor*, 1959 (Pls. 28, 37, 31), present full-length figures placed on an anonymous, monochromatic ground and display a more direct and controlled paint application. The importance of these paintings in Katz's development is their increased scale, both in format and in figures, and the restraint of gestural paint handling. The decrease in personalized gesture serves to abstract and generalize the subject, releasing its formal and typological potential. Katz's lack of attention to details of hands, feet, and clothing confirms his use of the figure as an abstract compositional device to be located on a two-dimensional ground in relation to the top and sides of the canvas, balancing color, weight, and scale. In this sense, the figures operate like the compositional elements of a Barnett Newman painting. In fact, the various Adas in this group—in white dress, in blue housecoat, in bathing suit—can be seen to function like Newman "zips."

Fig. 8
Franz Kline, *MAHONING*, 1956
Oil on canvas, 80 × 100 (203.2 × 254)
Whitney Museum of American Art, New York; purchase,
with funds from the Friends of the Whitney Museum
of American Art 57.10

Fig. 9
Larry Rivers, *DOUBLE PORTRAIT OF BERDIE*, 1955
Oil on canvas, 70¾ × 82½ (179.7 × 209.6)
Whitney Museum of American Art, New York; gift of
anonymous donor 56.49

The paintings of this period also seem to have benefited from the concepts Katz explored in the small cut-paper collages he began in 1955. These works represent tiny figures or objects cut out of painted paper and glued to a solid colored ground. The physical cutting and manipulation of the figures allowed Katz to test internal scale relationships and study effective figure, ground, and color relationships exclusive of subject matter. The collages also initially suggested to Katz the idea of a figure removed from the surface of a painting and the background, and resulted in the painted wood cutouts begun in 1959. Among these is one of Katz's first double portraits, *Ada Ada*, 1959 (Pl. 39). Double portraits had been done by Larry Rivers (Fig. 9), Katz's contemporary in age and impulse, but without Katz's bland, factual aggression. The dual, repetitive portrait afforded Katz another device to subvert the importance of the subject while enhancing the formal and generic presence of the image. A repeated Ada or Rauschenberg is jarring and illogical, and the redundancy actually tells us less than expected about the subject. The *Double Portrait of Robert Rauschenberg*, 1959 (Pl. 34), also makes reference to Rauschenberg's *Factum I* and *Factum II* (Figs. 10, 11), each of which contains a double portrait of Eisenhower. Rauschenberg's almost identical works proclaim that the apparent spontaneity of gesture, so crucial to Abstract Expressionist tenets, is inauthentic; and they share with Katz's work of this period a partial rejection of loose, personalized expressionism.

In the mid- and late 1950s, Rauschenberg, Johns, and Katz all sought to move away from the ambiguous, subconscious presentation of Abstract Expressionist work toward a more factual, controlled, and predetermined expression. Johns' choice of subjects—flags, targets, maps—are known, recognizable, impersonal images, and are conceptually aligned with Katz's interpretation of the human form. Katz's 1958–59 portraits begin to reduce the visible drips and the reliance on accident; what drips and gestures remain are intentional —a reminder of his debt to Abstract Expressionism and, at the same time, a way of announcing what is being rejected.

By the early 1960s, Katz had assimilated or rejected various aesthetic devices and concepts of the Abstract Expressionist, Color Field, and proto-Pop artists. His work now began to display more confidence, power, and skill. With paintings such as *Passing*, 1962–63, *Eli*, 1963, and *The Red Smile*, 1963 (Pls. 43, 46, 44), Katz made a big leap into larger scale, media-inspired horizontal formats and cropping, and an assured, smooth paint surface. His subjects became more impersonal, being executed in a flat, shallow space that further suppressed descriptive and painterly detail. Katz was attuned to the emerging aesthetic of the early 1960s. Along with Stella,

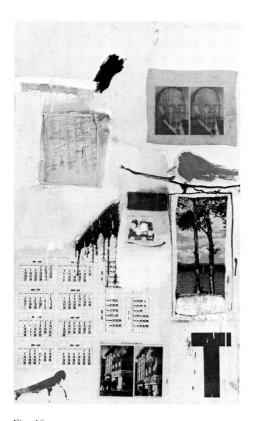

Fig. 10
Robert Rauschenberg, *FACTUM I*, 1957
Oil and collage on canvas, 62 × 35½ (157.5 × 90.2)
The Museum of Contemporary Art, Los Angeles; acquired from
the collection of Count Giuseppe Panza Di Biumo

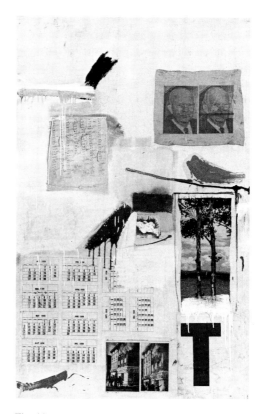

Fig. 11
Robert Rauschenberg, *FACTUM II*, 1957
Oil and collage on canvas, 62 × 35½ (157.5 × 90.2)
The Morton G. Neumann Family Collection

Kelly, Warhol, and Judd, he worked at making art that was emotionless—clear, reductive, and unambiguous. But for Katz, that goal was difficult because of the inherent content of portraiture and representational subject matter. To ease the problem, he looked to mass media—television, movies, advertising—for devices that would give his work increased clarity, high impact, compositional directness, and impersonality.

Visual symbols today are complicated by the movies, T.V., billboards, book reproductions, etc. They exert a continual pressure and in some cases, have taken the place of painting in that they have dominated our vision.... The media have also exerted influence on most high style figurative art and have in turn been influenced by fine art. [13]

Katz's statement acknowledges the dominant force of the media, and that advertising, in particular, offered him visual clues to picture making.

One media device that began to influence Katz's work in the early 1960s was a new form of billboard advertising. The 1950s were referred to as the "Golden Age of Paint" in the billboard business. [14] The hand-painted billboard replaced the illustrational and photographic paper paste-ups of earlier billboards to become the primary form of outdoor advertising. The painted billboard offered a larger, bolder image in stronger, more luminous colors. The speed and frequency with which

a new generation of consumers traveled on highways necessitated a larger scale for outdoor advertising and, during the 1950s, the size of the billboard increased to 14 by 48 feet. A face or product enlarged to that preposterous size became an arresting, eye-catching image, and the smallest detail grew more important and recognizable. The most often used device was a dramatically cropped face that loomed above the highway (Figs. 14–16). Cropping at the forehead or jawline was visually startling, making this huge face appear even larger, since it implied an unseen continuation. The concept of the image extending beyond the edge was, of course, occurring simultaneously in Abstract Expressionist painting, and was probably the source for advertising designers. But billboard design extended the idea further by attaching cutout plywood extensions to the rectangular form of the billboard. These overscale cutouts of smokers, beer bottles, or automobiles accentuated the surrealistic overtones already used in advertising, and gave the billboard a three-dimensional character by taking the image out of the painted plane and into the reality of the landscape or cityscape. It was this illusionistic and environmental aspect of advertising cutouts that had prompted Katz in 1959 to make his own cutouts. In his paintings, he adopted other characteristics of this new advertising age—large scale, intense flat color, gigantic cropped faces, and an absence of sen-

Fig. 12
James Rosenquist, *LOOK ALIVE (BLUE FEET)*, 1961
Oil on canvas with mirror, 67 × 58½ (170.2 × 148.6)
Collection of Michael D. Abrams

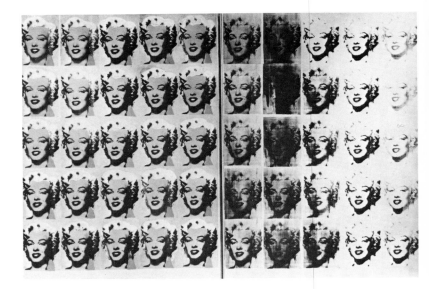

Fig. 13
Andy Warhol, *MARILYN MONROE DIPTYCH*, 1962
Oil on canvas, 82 × 114 (208.3 × 289.6)
The Tate Gallery, London

timentality—to achieve a modern representational art, at once fast and expansive, but devoid of the emotionalism of Abstract Expressionism and the overwrought narrative often contained in realist work. The same aggressive visual salesmanship that promotes the staples of American consumerism can be seen in Katz's depictions of *Eli*, 1963, *The Red Smile*, 1963, and *Paul Taylor*, 1964 (Pls. 46, 44, 50). They represent Katz's unique, Americanized brand of realism.

Katz's use of advertising techniques has been observed since the beginning of his career. In 1964 Irving Sandler noted that "Katz's portraits look singularly contemporary. By making them Gargantuan, he calls to mind enormous billboards. His approach to the human figure is a novel one, for he works on a scale seldom seen in art but familiar enough in our everyday life.... He does not simply re-create commercial art, but uses its impersonality as a contrast to the poignant intimacy imparted by his sitters.... The tension between Katz's love of tradition and his response to what he sees about him underlies his painting."[15] In a related comment, Edwin Denby found in Katz's work "the optic flash associated with advertising.... It upset the picture's weight—the rest of the painting couldn't keep up with its speed. Some Cubist and abstract pictures had caught the speed, but at the time representationalism could not."[16] But Katz had caught that speed by the early

1960s and harnessed its style and technique to evolve a similarly clean, quick, straightforward approach to painting.

An additional and related source for Katz were movies, which presented images in a grander, more stylish manner. Katz's use of the motion picture's close-up device is the most pronounced characteristic of his compositions. The large heads of *Ada with Bathing Cap*, 1965, *Swimmer #3*, 1973 (Pls. 47, 69), or the glamorous *Upside Down Ada*, 1965 (Pl. 51), are dramatically cropped, and situated on a horizontal field that aggressively pushes the image forward into the viewer's space. The enlarged and strongly lighted contours of the face, hair, and clothing allow Katz broad expanses of flat and smooth color, accentuating the largeness and visual impact of the form, as in *December*, 1979, and *Red Coat*, 1982 (Pls. 82, 90). Paintings such as these are often reminiscent of movie stills that freeze and isolate an image, and remove it from the narrative of a film. In addition, Katz uses this zoom lens approach to clarify, generalize, and idealize the countenance in order to make the image symbolic: "an art where the image and symbol are one.... to make a symbol that is clear as well as multiple; a symbol that can mean different things to different people, rather than a sign that is the same to all people."[17] It is here that Katz diverges radically from the Pop artists with whom he was prematurely and erro-

Fig. 14
Otis Shepard, billboard design for the
William Wrigley Jr. Company, 1950

Fig. 15
Haddon Sundblom, billboard design for the
Coca-Cola Company, 1951

Fig. 16
Coby Whitmore, billboard design for the
American Tobacco Company, 1953

Fig. 17
Michelangelo Antonioni, still from L'AVVENTURA, 1960

Fig. 18
Federico Fellini, still from LA DOLCE VITA, 1961

neously grouped, although they are related in their use of figurative elements and media-derived imagery. Andy Warhol's Campbell Soup cans or Marilyn Monroes (Fig. 13), for instance, are culturally and socially recognizable signs that have shared meaning in the public consciousness. In a similar way, James Rosenquist's direct borrowings of fragments of advertising imagery (Fig. 12) deliberately thwart any implied narrative because they are arranged in jarring juxtapositions that do not allow for romanticized or symbolic readings of the paintings.

Ada in *Blue Umbrella #2*, 1972 (Pl. 66), is surprisingly similar both in feeling and composition to a frame in Fellini's *La Dolce Vita* (Fig. 18) and, like the cinematic figure, is a singular, striking, and clear image that elicits multiple, ambiguous meanings. Ada can be read as a symbol of beauty, sorrow, mystery, coldness, or desire. In terms of physiognomic stylization, Ada also bears a striking resemblance to Elizabeth Taylor in a film still from *The Comedians* (Fig. 19). And when Ada appears in a car (*Impala*, 1968, *Ada and Vincent in the Car*, 1972 [Pls. 60, 64]), her portrait is imbued with the romance of the automobile and of the independent woman. Katz, in fact, has referred to *Impala* as "my Polish Rider,"[18] suggesting an analogy to Rembrandt's romantic and symbolic image of adventure and mystery. The possible meanings inherent in a Katz portrait are manifold and

the artist's strength lies in his deliberately ambiguous narrative—one without sentimentality and one that emphasizes appearance over meaning. The psychological content of some 1960s movies, such as Antonioni's study of ennui and alienation in *L'Avventura* (Fig. 17) or Bergman's *Persona* (Fig. 20), display the same coolness and distance as a Katz painting, the same supersession of style over content. This type of atmosphere was observed in a review of an early Katz exhibition that described the image of Ada "scoped and scaled like Antonioni, hardly more a presence than an impact on emptiness."[19]

But Alex Katz's work is, in fact, not empty, but full of formal, social, and psychological references, both historical and current. The resonance of Katz's art lies in its seamless amalgam of sources into his own distinct style. His work adroitly and intelligently synthesizes influences and impulses that emerge from and respond to the contemporary world: "I think of myself as a modern person and I want my painting to look that way. I think of my paintings as different from some others in that they derive a lot from modern paintings as well as from older paintings. . . . They're traditional because all painting belongs to the paintings before them, and they're modernistic because they're responsive to the immediate."[20]

Fig. 19
Peter Glenville, still from THE COMEDIANS, 1967

Fig. 20
Ingmar Bergman, still from PERSONA, 1967

Notes:

1. Quoted in Mark Strand, ed., *Art of the Real: Nine American Figurative Painters* (New York: Clarkson N. Potter, 1983), pp. 124, 129.

2. Quoted in Kate Horsfield, "On Art and Artists: Alex Katz," *Profile*, 2 (January 1982), p. 5.

3. Alex Katz, "Jackson Pollock: An Artists' Symposium, Part I," *Art News*, 66 (April 1967), p. 32.

4. Alex Katz, "Talk on Signs and Symbols," *ZZZZZZ*, ed. Kenward Elmslie (Calais, Vermont: Z Press, 1977), p. 23.

5. Quoted in Carter Ratcliff, "New York Today: Some Artists Comment," *Art in America*, 65 (September–October 1977), p. 82.

6. Françoise Cachin in *Manet 1832–1883*, exhibition catalogue (New York: The Metropolitan Museum of Art and Harry N. Abrams, 1983), p. 19.

7. Roberta Smith in *Alex Katz in the Seventies*, exhibition catalogue (Waltham, Massachusetts: Rose Art Museum, Brandeis University, 1978), pp. 13–14.

8. Quoted in Vincent Katz, "Plunk 'em Down and Paint' em," *The Ritz Newspaper*, no. 92 (1984), p. 59.

9. Alex Katz, "Talk on Signs and Symbols," p. 22.

10. Quoted in Ellen Schwartz, "Alex Katz: 'I See Something and Go Wow,'" *Art News*, 78 (Summer 1979), p. 45.

11. Ibid.

12. Frank O'Hara, "Alex Katz," *Art and Literature*, no. 9 (Summer 1966), pp. 91, 100.

13. Alex Katz, "Talk on Signs and Symbols," p. 26.

14. Sally Henderson and Robert Landau, *Billboard Art* (San Francisco: Chronicle Books, 1980), p. 48.

15. Irving Sandler, "In the Art Galleries," *The New York Post* (February 9, 1964), p. 40.

16. Edwin Denby, "Katz: Collage, Cutout, Cut-up," *Art News*, 63 (January 1965), p. 44.

17. Alex Katz, "Talk on Signs and Symbols," p. 23.

18. Alex Katz in conversation with the author, September 13, 1984.

19. Jack Kroll, "Reviews and Previews: Alex Katz," *Art News*, 61 (February 1963), p. 11.

20. Quoted in Strand, ed., *Art of the Real*, p. 132.

ALEX KATZ'S AMERICAN ACCENT

ROBERT ROSENBLUM

Becoming an artist in New York in the late fifties wasn't easy. If you wanted to be an abstract painter and were overwhelmed, and who wasn't, by the heroic grandeur of the greatest Abstract Expressionists, what could you do for an encore? And if, like Alex Katz, you were not only thrilled by the ambitious sweep and universal scale of a Pollock or a Newman, but also thought that commonplace sights like your friends' and family's faces, or the shoes and jackets they wore, were also worth putting on canvas, then things were even tougher. How could you get it all together in one painting? It must have seemed, at the time, that the gulf between the intangible, ideal realm of abstract art and the modest, here-and-now facts of everyday life was unbridgeable. But it turns out, as Katz went on to prove, that it wasn't. His work offers a stunning, indissoluble testimony to what must once have seemed an impossible marriage of the grand and the small, of the epic and the humble.

Take *February 5:30 PM*, 1972, or *Thursday Night #2* (Fig. 1). As their titles suggest, these are paintings that record ephemeral occasions, undramatic social gatherings that are casually clocked by the timepieces on wrist and wall rather than by the cosmic or psychological time of abstract art. The faces are of such individuality that even if we have not met the people, we almost feel an introduction is in order. In the same way, the clothing and hair styles are so time-bound that a later historian of costume could date the pictures quickly by observing the width of a lapel, the neckline of a sweater, the length

Fig. 1
Alex Katz, *THURSDAY NIGHT # 2*, 1974
Oil on canvas, 72 × 144 (182.9 × 365.8)
Collection of Paul Jacques Schupf

of someone's sideburns. But for all this matter-of-fact-ness, these groupings of men and women somehow exist as well in a noble, ideal realm that makes us blink away the specifics of date, place and name. The interior architecture itself—that of Katz's own loft—imposes, with its head-on view of window frames, the kind of lucid, rectilinear rhythms we feel regulating the spaces of the most dignified Old Master compositions; and the figures too, we realize, follow the subliminal beat of these strong parallel and perpendicular harmonies. Although these people may at first seem to be as easy in their stances as guests at a cocktail party, at second glance, the subtle locking of certain heads and bodies into frontal or profile views freezes the groups as a whole in a serene and unchangeable order. It's as if the noble figures who populate the ideal perspective spaces of those Renaissance paintings Katz has always loved and studied had miraculously been resurrected in the New York of the 1970s and relocated in the architectural spaces of a SoHo loft building.

Even the rendering of details of faces and clothing shares this dual allegiance to present fact and venerable pictorial traditions. For however recognizably Katz records the woven pattern of a tie or skirt, or the exact fall of someone's flowing hair, the level of visual generalization is surprisingly high, with the textures of skin or wall of equal smoothness and the definition of any contour

Fig. 2
Alex Katz, *EDWIN*, 1972
Oil on canvas, 96¼ × 72¼ (244.5 × 183.5)
Marlborough Gallery Inc., New York

Fig. 3
Alex Katz, *TRIO*, 1975
Oil on canvas, 72 × 96 (182.9 × 243.8)
Private collection

—be it hairline or window blind—of the same, silhouetted crispness. Indeed, in *Thursday Night #2*, the painted figure of Katz's wife, Ada, in the painting within the painting (on the right wall) belongs to the same realm of abstraction as the presumably "real" figures in the foreground. The instant effect of an almost candid-camera truth slowly disappears and we find that this seeming realism is everywhere belied, in both the whole and the parts. What begins as a way of seeing that can be literal enough to record, as in *Edwin* (Fig. 2), the most particular facts of close-up physiognomy or, as in *Roof Garden* (Fig. 12), the very brand name (Vantage) of two packages of cigarettes on a sunlit table, is uncannily transformed into a still, imperturbable world that is simultaneously rooted in, but remote from, our prosaic environment.

It is fascinating to watch this phenomenon at work. In *Trio* (Fig. 3), Katz grasps the spectator's attention instantly with a characteristic device. The three young women are virtually life-size, and they appear to be casually cropped by the frame at hair, elbow and one shoulder, with one bluntly foreshortened arm extending a water glass outward toward the viewer. We feel that they must be invading our space as we are theirs. Even the light seems to belong to both their world and ours; for it comes from outside the picture on the left, then enters the painted image to glisten for a moment on the

two half-filled glasses and a necklace of blue beads, and finally disappears offstage to the right. Moreover, the intricate rainbow weave of the knit sweater is fussy and detailed enough to vouch for on-the-spot visual truth. Yet slowly, the same space, figures, and clothing take on an ever greater distance from the beholder's world. The deep blue monochrome background, whose purity permits no objects or brush marks, leads us to an abstract, spaceless realm; and the light, if shimmering here and there, is suddenly crystallized forever in the broad, clean divisions of luminous against shadowed planes. And with this, the profile and frontal postures again stop the movement of time and space, so that finally, these three young women—Rosalie, Laurie and Jane—almost seem the contemporary descendants of the Three Graces or perhaps of a trio of silent, motionless saints who stand forever in the limpid geometric spaces of a Quattrocento altarpiece. Unexpectedly, the casual becomes solemn, and even the grave, stepwise ascent of hands on glasses takes on a ritual character.

Throughout Katz's work, the most ordinary, humdrum sights can take on an almost iconic quality. Who but Katz would have chosen to paint, from the experience of an American summer vacation, an empty canoe? And who else would expand it to life-size dimensions across a 12-foot canvas, and then float it horizontally on a symbolic sea of abstract blue water (Pl. 72)?

Fig. 4
Thomas Eakins, *THE PAIR-OARED SHELL (THE OARSMEN)*, 1872
Oil on canvas, 24 × 36½ (61 × 92.7)
Philadelphia Museum of Art; given by Mrs. Thomas Eakins and
Miss Mary Adeline Williams

Fig. 5
Alex Katz, *GOOD AFTERNOON # 2*, 1974
Oil on canvas, 72 × 96 (182.9 × 243.8)
Collection of Paul Jacques Schupf

Both as real and unreal as its almost, but not quite unbroken reflection in the still water, the canoe delights and awes us by transforming a lakeside commonplace into an object of mysterious fixity, eternally moored in a horizonless space. Even when the canoe is manned and navigated toward a horizon, as in *Good Afternoon #2* (Fig. 5), the same spell is cast. The slight irregularities of the coastline and the tilt of the canoe and paddler (typical Katz observations of authentic fact versus arbitrary order) suddenly click into place in a seemingly effortless junction of near and far, parallel and perpendicular. The leisure rhythms of summer have been magically immobilized and preserved in a broad design which, like Katz's simplified modeling in clean-hewn planes, is at once innocent and artful.

In these canoeing scenes, with their quality of plain statements about plain truths, we are often reminded of an American pictorial tradition, harking back, in this case, to those still and silent boating pictures by George Caleb Bingham and William Sidney Mount, which reach their nineteenth-century climax in Thomas Eakins' own paintings of real people in real sculls pinpointed for all time on the watery, but opaque planes of the Schuylkill River (Fig. 4). And in this domain, Katz's work can even make us see freshly the likes of Frederic Remington, whose large American idyll, *Coming to the Call* (Fig. 6), offers surprising previews of Katz's Maine vacation scenes, not only in the sharp, reductive pattern of the canoe and its reflection against water, earth, and sky, but even in the spiky silhouettes of a moose and his antlers, observed with the same startling insouciance as Katz's own close-up encounter with the rear of a moose that has suddenly turned toward the spectator (Fig. 7). And thinking of the American character of Katz's art, the spirit of more naive folk traditions is also evoked in his straightforward presentation of people, things, and places, and in his brusque assertion of palpable fact by a kind of whittled opposition of light and dark surfaces against a flatly patterned ground, a device familiar in the less sophisticated territories of American art, from Colonial portraiture to signboard painting and painted wooden figures and animals. At times, we might even think that had the Douanier Rousseau been raised in New York City and had spent his summers in Maine, his pictures might not have looked too different from Katz's.

Nevertheless, this veneer of innocence covers an enormous pictorial sophistication and Katz's paintings stir up countless sources and references to grander European traditions. As those who know him can attest, Katz talks enthusiastically and knowledgeably about all the Old Masters, making his points with this Giotto or that Velázquez, and constantly adjusting his own art to their lofty standards. In general, though, it is the domain

Fig. 6
Frederic Remington, *COMING TO THE CALL*, 1905
Oil on canvas, 27¼ × 40¼ (69.2 × 102.2)
Private collection

Fig. 7
Alex Katz, *MOOSE HORN STATE PARK*, 1975
Oil on canvas, 78 × 144 (198.1 × 365.8)
Marlborough Gallery Inc., New York

Fig. 8
Gustave Caillebotte, *PARIS, A RAINY DAY (INTERSECTION OF THE RUE DE TURIN AND THE RUE DE MOSCOU)*, 1877
Oil on canvas, 83½ × 108¾ (212.1 × 276.2)
The Art Institute of Chicago; Charles H. and Mary F. S. Worcester Fund

Fig. 10
Alex Katz, *ISLESBORO FERRYSLIP*, 1976
Oil on canvas, 78 × 84 (198.1 × 213.4)
Collection of Paul Jacques Schupf

Fig. 9
Edgar Degas, *VICOMTE LEPIC AND HIS DAUGHTERS (PLACE DE LA CONCORDE)*, 1875
Oil on canvas, 31⅛ × 47⅛ (79 × 119.7)
Destroyed

of Impressionism that offers the most obvious transatlantic counterparts to Katz's vision; and, in particular, it is the likes of Degas and Caillebotte, with their mastery of cropping, of asymmetrical order, of flash-freeze monumentality, whom Katz most often conjures up. *Islesboro Ferryslip* (Fig. 10), in its rhythmically measured pier that plunges us swiftly from a close-up to the remote distance and in its seemingly casual confrontation with figures walking out of the picture into our space, has many French ancestors of the 1870s, recalling devices used by Caillebotte a century before in, among other works, the now famous Chicago painting, *Paris, a Rainy Day* (Fig. 8), or by Degas in the portrait of the *Vicomte Lepic and His Daughters* (Fig. 9). But the flavor is again that of an American translation, in which softness of atmosphere, delicacy of surface are replaced by a no-nonsense clarity of light and texture.

The point is made even more strongly when Katz depicts scenes familiar in popular memory from the Impressionist repertory of sunstruck leisure. In *Roof Garden* (Fig. 12), a double portrait of John Button and Clark Bott enjoying the rooftop of their SoHo loft, the summery world of Manet, Monet and Renoir is transported from the 1870s to the 1970s and from the suburbs of Paris to the urban core of New York's art scene. Renoir's *Rowers' Lunch* (Fig. 11) provides only one of many French counterparts, where dappled sunlight crosses a

Fig. 11
Pierre Auguste Renoir, *ROWERS' LUNCH*, 1879–80
Oil on canvas, 21½ × 25½ (54.6 × 64.8)
The Art Institute of Chicago; Potter Palmer
Collection

Fig. 12
Alex Katz, *ROOF GARDEN*, 1975
Oil on canvas, 72 × 96 (182.9 × 243.8)
Collection of Paul Jacques Schupf

trellis pattern and spills over a convivial scene in which smoke and drink contribute to the general détente of mind and muscle. But in Katz's translation of this familiar Impressionist ambience, an American accent again rings clear. Contours are tough and clean, postures of relaxation are frozen, and even the squares of light that float onto the sitters and spot their hair and clothing have as harsh and stubborn a reality as the paired packs of Vantage cigarettes. The fragrant dissolution in the Renoir reverses gears, transforming Impressionist idylls of sensual blur and comfort into an almost Puritanical alertness and rigor that would not be alien to the Colonial portrait milieu of Copley himself.

As for these pervasive American qualities, it should be said, finally, that Katz's paintings, in the long run, feel most at home with the sophisticated, mainline traditions of American art since 1945. The sheer scale and simplification of his images, with their vast expanses of flat, unbroken color (whether of a lake or of a cheek), join forces both with the most daring inventions of abstract painting in the 1950s and with the kind of billboard-size imagery many Pop artists explored in the next decade. Yet Katz fits into neither category. His absorption of the structural boldness of such masters as Newman is always at the service of making us see the poetry of the ordinary, and never denies the priority of homely detail. And his view of the commonplace, while

often attuned to the public, urban scale of Lichtenstein's or Rosenquist's Pop icons, is not an image of social or aesthetic irony, but rather a loving, directly perceived record of the sweet facts of the people and places that provide the continuities of the artist's life. What may finally be most remarkable about Katz's achievement is the way in which he has taken the stuff of daily living and loving we thought suitable only for an uneventful diary entry and transferred it, without a manifesto, to the grand-scale arena of American monumental painting today. Both private and public, modest and proud, these commanding pictures fuse the highest demands of ambitious abstract art with the need to record the quiet truths of personal experience.

PAINTINGS

CUTOUTS

COLLAGES

Pl. 1. *Winter Scene*, 1951–52
Oil on board, 24 × 24 (61 × 61)
Collection of the artist

Pl. 2. *Four Children*, 1951–52
Oil on board, 18 × 18 (45.7 × 45.7)
Collection of Jean Cohen

Pl. 3. *After Softball*, 1953
Oil on board, 24 × 24 (61 × 61)
Collection of the artist

Pl. 4. *Two Trees*, 1955
Oil on board, 32 × 32 (81.3 × 81.3)
Robert Miller Gallery, New York

Pl. 5. *Two Figures*, 1954
Oil on board, 32 × 32 (81.3 × 81.3)
Collection of the artist

Pl. 6. *Ives Field*, 1956
Oil on board, 32 × 32 (81.3 × 81.3)
Robert Miller Gallery, New York

40

Pl. 7. *Track Jacket*, 1956
Oil on board, 24 × 18 (61 × 45.7)
Collection of the artist

Pl. 8. *Man with Dog*, 1955
Collage, 4 × 6 (10.2 × 15.2)
Collection of Roy Leaf

Pl. 9. *Two Figures*, 1955
Collage, 4 × 6 (10.2 × 15.2)
Collection of the artist

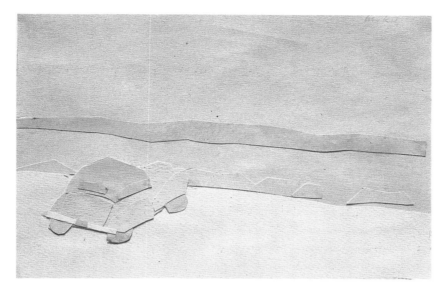

Pl. 10. *Roadmaster*, 1955–56
Collage, 4½ × 7 (11.4 × 17.8)
Collection of the artist

Pl. 11. *Pink Beach*, 1956
Collage, 5 × 7 (12.7 × 17.8)
Collection of Sanford Schwartz

Pl. 12. *Two Figures at Lincolnville Beach*, 1956–57
Collage, 5 × 8 (12.7 × 20.3)
Collection of the artist

Pl. 13. *Raft*, 1956
Collage, 5 × 8 (12.7 × 20.3)
Robert Miller Gallery, New York

Pl. 14. *Three People*, 1957
Collage, 4 × 6 (10.2 × 15.2)
Robert Miller Gallery, New York

Pl. 15. *Beach House*, 1959
Collage, 5 × 7 (12.7 × 17.8)
Collection of the artist

Pl. 16. *Sunset Cove*, 1957
Collage, 4 × 6 (10.2 × 15.2)
Collection of Jane Freilicher and Joseph Hazan

Pl. 17. *Bathers*, 1959
Collage, 4 × 6 (10.2 × 15.2)
Collection of Mr. and Mrs. Fayez Sarofim

Pl. 18. *Ada in the Water*, 1958
Collage, 5 × 8 (12.7 × 20.3)
Collection of Alice and Leo Yamin

Pl. 19. *Sleeping Figure*, 1959
Collage, 4¼ × 6½ (10.8 × 16.5)
Collection of Mr. and Mrs. Fayez Sarofim

Pl. 20. *Greenwood Lake, New Jersey*, 1960
Collage, 13¼ × 15⅝ (33.7 × 39.7)
International Council of The Museum of Modern Art,
New York

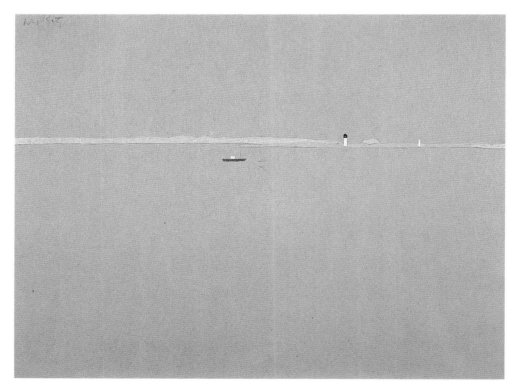

Pl. 21. *Twilight*, 1960
Collage, 13⅞ × 15⅝ (35.2 × 39.7)
International Council of The Museum of Modern Art,
New York

Pl. 22. *Dog at End of Pier*, 1960
Collage, 8½ × 11¼ (21.6 × 28.6)
Collection of Peter R. Stern

Pl. 23. *Olives*, 1955
Collage, 8½ × 11 (21.6 × 27.9)
Robert Miller Gallery, New York

Pl. 24. *Blueberry Field # 1*, 1959
Collage, 14 × 17 (35.6 × 43.2)
Collection of the artist

Pl. 25. *Provincetown*, 1971
Collage, 18 × 24 (45.7 × 61)
Robert Miller Gallery, New York

Pl. 26. *Ada in Black Sweater*, 1957
Oil on board, 24 × 18 (61 × 45.7)
Robert Miller Gallery, New York

Pl. 27. *Self-Portrait (Cigarette)*, 1957
Oil on board, 36 × 24 (91.4 × 61)
Robert Miller Gallery, New York

Pl. 28. *Irving and Lucy*, 1958
Oil on canvas, 60 × 60 (152.4 × 152.4)
Collection of Irving and Lucy Sandler

Pl. 29. *Ada in White Dress*, 1958
Oil on canvas, 60 × 48 (152.4 × 121.9)
Collection of Mr. and Mrs. Jack N. Greenman

Pl. 30. *Eli at Ducktrap*, 1958
Oil on canvas, 49 × 71 (124.5 × 180.3)
Private collection

Pl. 31. *Paul Taylor*, 1959
Oil on canvas, 72 × 84 (182.9 × 213.4)
Collection of the artist

Pl. 32. *Blackie Walking*, 1959
Oil on board cutouts, four figures,
10¾ × 16¼ (27.3 × 41.3) overall
Hirshl & Adler Modern, New York

Pl. 33. *Frank O'Hara*, 1959–60
Oil on wood cutout, 60 × 15 (152.4 × 38.1)
Collection of Elaine de Kooning

Pl. 34. *Double Portrait of Robert Rauschenberg*, 1959
Oil on canvas, 66 × 85½ (167.6 × 217.2)
Collection of Paul Jacques Schupf

Pl. 35. *Norman Bluhm*, 1959
Oil on canvas, 48 × 48 (121.9 × 121.9)
Collection of Paul Jacques Schupf

Pl. 36. *Ada in Blue Housecoat*, 1959
Oil on canvas, 80 × 50 (203.2 × 127)
The Rivendell Collection

Pl. 37. *Bather*, 1959
Oil on canvas, 48 × 72 (121.9 × 182.9)
Collection of the artist

Pl. 38. *Portrait of Joe*, 1961
Oil on wood cutout, 45¾ × 16⅜ (116.2 × 41.6)
Everhart Museum, Scranton, Pennsylvania

Pl. 39. *Ada Ada*, 1959
Oil on wood cutout, 39 × 22 (99.1 × 55.9)
Collection of the artist

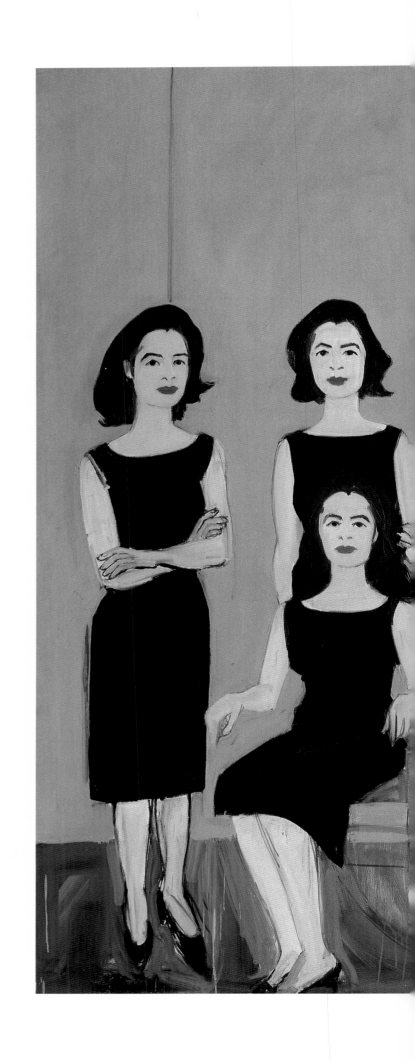

Pl. 40. *The Black Dress*, 1960
Oil on canvas, 72 × 84 (182.9 × 213.4)
Collection of the artist

Pl. 41. *Luna Park*, 1960
Oil on canvas, 40 × 30 (101.6 × 76.2)
Collection of the artist

Pl. 42. *October # 2*, 1962
Oil on canvas, 59 × 49 (149.9 × 124.5)
Robert Miller Gallery, New York

Pl. 43. *Passing*, 1962–63
Oil on canvas, 72¾ × 79⅝ (182.2 × 202.2)
The Museum of Modern Art, New York; Gift of the Louis
and Bessie Adler Foundation Inc., Seymour M. Klein, President

Pl. 44. *The Red Smile*, 1963
Oil on canvas, 78¾ × 114¾ (200 × 292.1)
Whitney Museum of American Art, New York; Purchase,
with funds from the Painting and Sculpture Committee 83.3

Pl. 45. *View*, 1962
Oil on canvas, 30 × 40 (76.2 × 101.6)
Collection of Rudolph Burckhardt

Pl. 46. *Eli*, 1963
Oil on canvas, 72 × 86 (182.9 × 218.4)
Whitney Museum of American Art, New York; Gift of
Mr. and Mrs. Herbert Fischbach 64.37

Pl. 47. *Ada with Bathing Cap*, 1965
Oil on canvas, 60 × 72 (152.4 × 182.9)
Collection of Paul Jacques Schupf

Pl. 48. *Alex*, 1968
Oil on aluminum cutout, 71 × 18½ (180.3 × 47)
Collection of the artist

Pl. 49. *The Cocktail Party*, 1965
Oil on canvas, 72 × 96 (182.9 × 243.8)
Collection of Paul Jacques Schupf

Pl. 50. *Paul Taylor*, 1964
Oil on canvas, 60 × 60 (152.4 × 152.4)
Collection of Charles and Stephanie Reinhart

80

Pl. 51. *Upside Down Ada*, 1965
Oil on canvas, 52 × 63 (132.1 × 160)
Collection of the artist

Pl. 52. *White Lilies*, 1966
Oil on canvas, 93 × 79½ (236.2 × 201.9)
Milwaukee Art Museum; Gift of Jane Bradley Pettit

Pl. 53. *Ada with Superb Lily*, 1967
Oil on canvas, 46½ × 52 (118.1 × 132.1)
The Herbert W. Plimpton Collection on extended loan to the
Rose Art Museum, Brandeis University, Waltham, Massachusetts

Pl. 54. *Swamp Maple, 4:30*, 1968
Oil on canvas, 144 × 93 (365.8 × 236.2)
Collection of the artist

Pl. 55. *Ada and Vincent*, 1967
Oil on canvas, 95 × 72 (241.3 × 182.9)
Collection of the artist

Pl. 56. *Rudy and Edwin*, 1968
Oil on aluminum cutout, 48 × 43½ (121.9 × 110.5)
Collection of the artist

Pl. 57. *Ada Four Times*, 1968
Oil on aluminum cutout, 50½ × 33 (128.3 × 83.8)
Collection of Dr. and Mrs. Terry Podolsky

Pl. 58. *One Flight Up*, 1968 (front and back)
Oil on aluminum cutouts,
67¾ × 180 × 47 (172.1 × 457.2 × 119.4) overall
Robert Miller Gallery, New York

Pl. 59. *Ada with Nose*, 1969–70
Oil on aluminum cutout, 71½ × 72 (181.6 × 182.9)
Collection of the artist

Pl. 60. *Impala*, 1968
Oil on canvas, 72 × 109 (182.9 × 276.9)
The Cleveland Museum of Art; Purchase Mr. and Mrs. William H. Marlatt Fund and
Gift of The Eppler Family Foundation and Agnes Gund Saalfield

Pl. 61. *Sunny*, 1971
Oil on canvas, 96¼ × 72¼ (244.5 × 183.5)
Milwaukee Art Museum; Gift of Mrs. Harry Lynde Bradley

Pl. 62. *Vincent and Tony*, 1969
Oil on canvas, 72½ × 120⅞ (184.2 × 307)
The Art Institute of Chicago; Gift of
The Society for Contemporary Art

Pl. 63. *Walk*, 1970
Oil on canvas, 72 × 144 (182.9 × 365.8)
Collection of the artist

Pl. 64. *Ada and Vincent in the Car*, 1972
Oil on canvas, 72 × 96 (182.9 × 243.8)
Hirshhorn Museum and Sculpture Garden,
Smithsonian Institution, Washington, D.C.

Pl. 65. *Self-Portrait with Sunglasses*, 1969
Oil on canvas, 96 × 68 (243.8 × 172.7)
Virginia Museum of Fine Arts, Richmond;
Gift of Sydney and Frances Lewis

Pl. 66. *Blue Umbrella # 2*, 1972
Oil on canvas, 96 × 144 (243.8 × 365.8)
Collection of Paul Jacques Schupf

Pl. 67. *The Black Jacket*, 1972
Oil on canvas, 78 × 144 (198.1 × 365.8)
Collection of Paul Jacques Schupf

Pl. 68. *Vincent with Radio*, 1974
Oil on canvas, 76 × 96 (193 × 243.8)
Collection of Susan Merians

Pl. 69. *Swimmer # 3*, 1973
Oil on canvas, 60 × 72 (152.4 × 182.9)
Collection of Paul Jacques Schupf

Pl. 70. *Good Afternoon # 2*, 1974
Oil on canvas, 72 × 96 (182.9 × 243.8)
Collection of Paul Jacques Schupf

Pl. 71. *Roof Garden*, 1975
Oil on canvas, 72 × 96 (182.9 × 243.8)
Collection of Paul Jacques Schupf

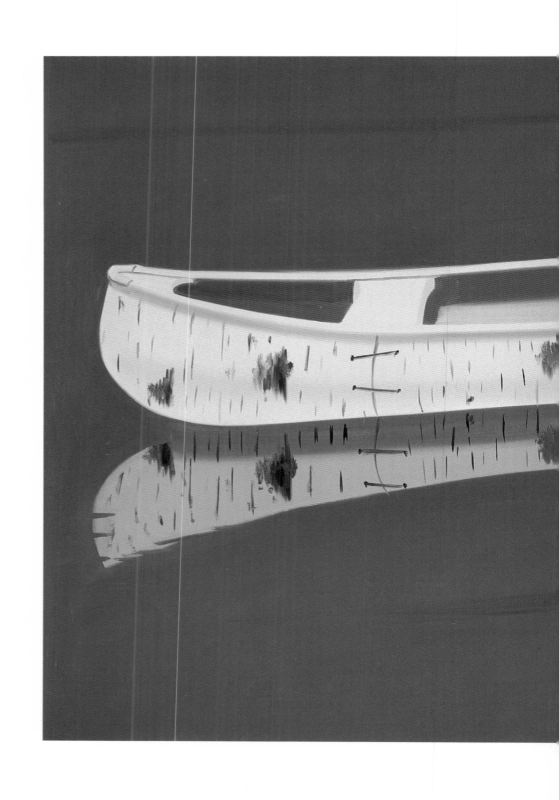

Pl. 72. *Canoe*, 1974
Oil on canvas, 72 × 144 (182.9 × 365.8)
Atlantic Richfield Corporate Art Collection, Los Angeles

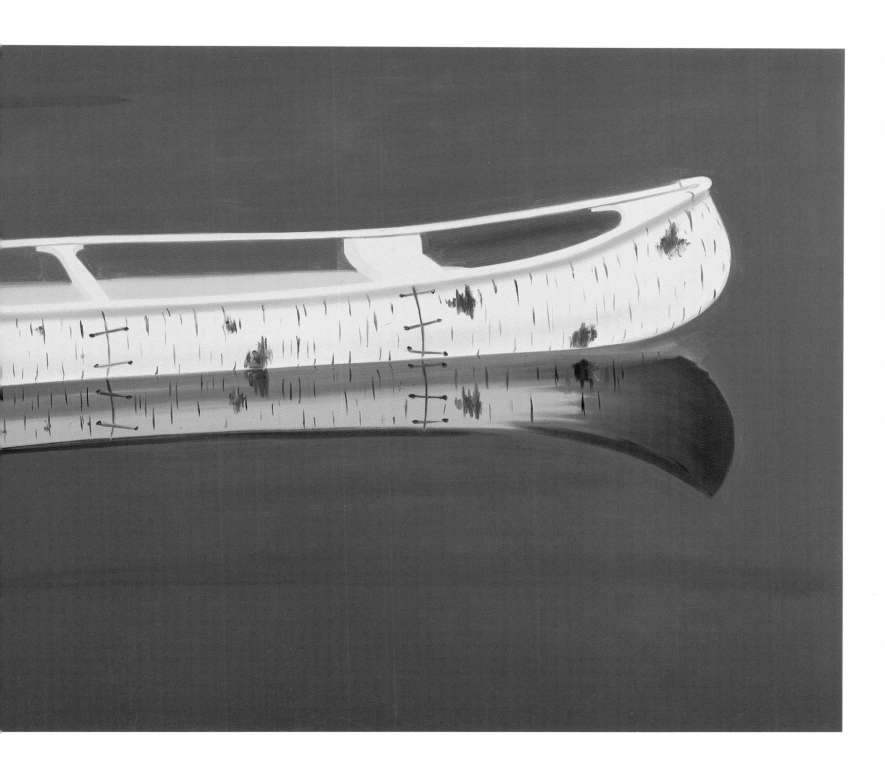

Pl. 73. *Moose Horn State Park*, 1975
Oil on canvas, 78 × 144 (198.1 × 365.8)
Marlborough Gallery Inc., New York

Pl. 74. *Twilight*, 1975
Oil on canvas, 126 × 96 (320 × 243.8)
Marlborough Gallery Inc., New York

Pl. 75. *Night*, 1976
Oil on canvas, 72 × 96 (182.9 × 243.8)
Pennsylvania Academy of the Fine Arts, Philadelphia;
Contemporary Arts Purchase Fund

Pl. 76. *Thursday Night # 2*, 1974
Oil on canvas, 72 × 144 (182.9 × 365.8)
Collection of Paul Jacques Schupf

Pl. 77. *Islesboro Ferryslip*, 1976
Oil on canvas, 78 × 84 (198.1 × 213.4)
Collection of Paul Jacques Schupf

Pl. 78. *Place*, 1977
Oil on canvas, 108 × 144 (274.3 × 365.8)
Whitney Museum of American Art, New York;
Gift of Sydney and Frances Lewis 78.23

Pl. 79. *Round Hill*, 1977
Oil on canvas, 72 × 96 (182.9 × 243.8)
Private collection

Pl. 80. *His Behind the Back Pass*, 1979
Oil on canvas, 72 × 96 (182.9 × 243.8)
Marlborough Gallery Inc., New York

Pl. 81. *The Yellow House*, 1982
Oil on canvas, 78 × 72 (198.1 × 182.9)
Marlborough Gallery Inc., New York

Pl. 82. *December*, 1979
Oil on canvas, 132 × 108 (335.3 × 274.3)
Marlborough Gallery Inc., New York

Pl. 83. *John*, 1982
Oil on aluminum cutout, 36 × 4 (91.4 × 10.2)
Robert Miller Gallery, New York

Pl. 84. *Ada*, 1982
Oil on aluminum cutout, 36 × 4 (91.4 × 10.2)
Collection of the artist

Pl. 85. *Marcia*, 1982
Oil on aluminum cutout, 36 × 4 (91.4 × 10.2)
Robert Miller Gallery, New York

Pl. 86. *Rudy*, 1979
Oil on aluminum cutout, 72 × 10 (182.9 × 25.4)
Collection of the artist

Pl. 87. *Sanford Schwartz*, 1978
Oil on aluminum cutout, 71 × 10 (180.3 × 25.4)
Collection of Dr. and Mrs. Marvin H. Rivkin

Pl. 88. *Ada (Black and White Dress)*, 1980
Oil on aluminum cutout, 69¼ × 4 (175.9 × 10.2)
Mira Godard Gallery, Toronto

Pl. 89. *Ada and Alex*, 1980
Oil on canvas, 60 × 72 (152.4 × 182.9)
Collection of Alan P. Safir

Pl. 90. *Red Coat*, 1982
Oil on canvas, 96 × 48 (243.8 × 121.9)
Collection of Leslie and Stanley Westreich

Pl. 91. *Pas de Deux*, 1983
Oil on canvas, five panels, 132 × 360 (335.3 × 914.4) overall
Collection of Paul Jacques Schupf

Pl. 92. *Bathers (Vincent and Anastasia)*, 1984
Oil on aluminum cutout, 68 × 45 (172.7 × 114.3)
Robert Miller Gallery, New York

Pl. 93. *Sunset (Christopher and Kate)*, 1984
Oil on aluminum cutout, 69½ × 47½ (176.5 × 120.7)
Robert Miller Gallery, New York

Pl. 94. *Eleuthera*, 1984
Oil on canvas, four panels, 120 × 264 (304.8 × 670.6) overall
Marlborough Gallery Inc., New York

SELECTED EXHIBITIONS

ONE-MAN EXHIBITIONS

1954
Roko Gallery, New York. "Alex Katz: Paintings."
   October 18–November 16.

1957
Roko Gallery, New York. "Alex Katz: Paintings." January 7–30.

1958
The Sun Gallery, Provincetown, Massachusetts. "Alex Katz."

1959
Tanager Gallery, New York. "Alex Katz." January 16–February 6.
   Exhibition catalogue, foreword by Irving Sandler.

1960
Stable Gallery, New York. "Alex Katz." March 15–April 2.

1961
Stable Gallery, New York. "Alex Katz." February 20–March 11.
Mili-Jay Gallery, Woodstock, New York. "Alex Katz: Recent
   Paintings." July 22–August 3.

1962
Tanager Gallery, New York. "Alex Katz: Flat Statues."
   February 9–March 1.
Martha Jackson Gallery, New York. "Alex Katz: The Set for
   'George Washington Crossing the Delaware.'" June 5–30.

1963
Thibaut Gallery, New York. "Alex Katz." February 12–March 9.

1964
Fischbach Gallery, New York. "Alex Katz." January 28–
   February 22.

1965
Fischbach Gallery, New York. "Alex Katz: Cut-outs—
   1955–65." January 5–30.

Fischbach Gallery, New York. "Alex Katz: Paintings." November 23–December 26.

1966

David Stuart Gallery, Los Angeles. "Alex Katz."

1967

Fischbach Gallery, New York. "Alex Katz: Cut-outs." January 7–February 4.

Fischbach Gallery, New York. "Alex Katz." December 2, 1967–January 5, 1968

1968

Fischbach Gallery, New York. "Alex Katz." October 26–November 4.

1969

Mont Chateau Lodge, West Virginia University, Morgantown. Presented by West Virginia University and the West Virginia Arts and Humanities Council. "Alex Katz at Cheat Lake." August 1–31. Exhibition catalogue, introduction by Scott Burton.

Phyllis Kind Gallery, Chicago. "Alex Katz."

1970

Fischbach Gallery, New York. "Alex Katz: New Paintings." September 26–October 22.

1971

Utah Museum of Fine Arts, University of Utah, Salt Lake City. "Alex Katz." January 7–February 7. Traveled to The Art Gallery, University of California, San Diego, February 22–April 14; Minnesota Museum of Art, St. Paul, July 16–October 3; Wadsworth Atheneum, Hartford, November 10–December 31. Exhibition catalogue, preface by Irving Sandler; essays by William Berkson, Lucy Lippard, Robert Rosenblum, David Antin, Ron Padgett; "Selected Writings about Katz," edited by Irving Sandler and William Berkson.

Galerie Brusberg, Hannover, West Germany. "Alex Katz." January 9–February 20.

Phyllis Kind Gallery, Chicago. "Alex Katz: Cut-outs—Paintings." January–February.

Fischbach Gallery, New York. "Alex Katz: Prints." May 25–June 21.

Fischbach Gallery, New York. "Alex Katz: Cut-outs." October 22–November 11.

Galerie Thelen, Cologne, West Germany. "Alex Katz."

1972

Reed College Art Gallery, Portland, Oregon. "Alex Katz." April 5–28.

1973

Ässä Galleria, Helsinki, Finland. "The American Neo-Realist: Alex Katz." November 2–13. Exhibition catalogue, introduction by Sakari Saarikivi.

Marlborough Gallery Inc., New York. "Alex Katz." December 8–29. Exhibition catalogue, introduction by Carter Ratcliff.

1974

The Picker Art Gallery, Charles A. Dana Creative Arts Center, Colgate University, Hamilton, New York. "Alex Katz: Recent Works from the Collection of Paul J. Schupf." January 20–February 17. Exhibition catalogue, foreword by Edward Bryant; introduction by Paul J. Schupf.

Marlborough Godard Gallery, Toronto. "Alex Katz." February 9–March 2.

Davison Art Center, Wesleyan University, Middletown, Connecticut. "Alex Katz." March 9–April 21. Exhibition catalogue, introduction by Richard S. Field.

Whitney Museum of American Art, New York. "Alex Katz Prints." September 9–October 26. Traveled to Virginia Museum of Fine Arts, Richmond, January 10–February 9, 1975; Utah Museum of Fine Arts, Salt Lake City, February 17–March 31, 1975; The Santa Barbara Museum of Art, California, April 7–May 19, 1975; University Gallery, University of Minnesota, Minneapolis, July 20–August 24, 1975; Indianapolis Museum of Art, September 2–October 12, 1975. Exhibition catalogue, essays by Richard S. Field and Elke M. Solomon.

1975

Marlborough Fine Art Ltd., London. "Alex Katz." January 28–February 21.

Galerie Arnesen, Copenhagen. "Alex Katz." March 7–April 9.

Galerie Marguérite Lamy, Paris. "Alex Katz: Recent Works." May 29–July 12. Exhibition catalogue.

Marlborough Gallery Inc., New York. "Alex Katz: Exhibition of Graphics 1972–75." December 6–27.

1976

Marlborough Gallery Inc., New York. "Alex Katz: Recent Works." February 28–March 20. Exhibition catalogue.

Marlborough Godard Gallery, Toronto. "Alex Katz: Recent Works." April 10–May 10.

Benjamin Mangel Gallery, Bala Cynwyd, Pennsylvania. "Alex Katz: Exhibition of Graphics 1972–75." May 1–30.

1977

Fresno Arts Center and Museum, California. "Alex Katz: Recent Paintings." September 7–October 9. Traveled to Art Galleries, California State University, Long Beach, October 17–November 6; Seattle Art Museum, November 17, 1977–January 8, 1978; Vancouver Art Gallery, British Columbia, Canada, February 4–March 5, 1978. Exhibition catalogue, introduction by R. Andrew Maass; essay by Robert Rosenblum.

Galerie Roger d'Amécourt, Paris. "Alex Katz." October 11–November 12. Exhibition catalogue, introduction by Roger d'Amécourt.

Marlborough Galerie AG, Zurich. "Alex Katz." December 8, 1977–January 27, 1978.

1978

Marlborough Gallery Inc., New York. "Alex Katz: Recent Paintings." February 24–March 25. Exhibition catalogue.

Richard Eugene Fuller Art Gallery, Beaver College, Glendale, Pennsylvania. "Alex Katz." April 5–21.

Mira Godard Gallery, Toronto. "Alex Katz: Recent Paintings." April 15–May 6.

Susanne Hilberry Gallery, Birmingham, Michigan. "Alex Katz." April 29–May 31.

Hokin Gallery, Chicago. "Alex Katz: Paintings." May 12–June 20.

Rose Art Museum, Brandeis University, Waltham, Massachusetts. "Alex Katz in the Seventies." May 27–July 9. Exhibition catalogue, preface by Carl Belz; essay by Roberta Smith.

Benjamin Mangel Gallery, Philadelphia. "Alex Katz and His Beautiful People." November 1–30.

Wilcox Gallery, Swarthmore College, Swarthmore, Pennsylvania. "Alex Katz: Selected Prints." November 30–December 21.

1979

Weatherspoon Art Gallery, University of North Carolina, Greensboro. "Alex Katz: Prints." January 14–February 4.

Brooke Alexander Gallery, New York. "Alex Katz: *Face of the Poet*." February 10–March 10. Exhibition catalogue, poems by Ted Berrigan, Kenward Elmslie, John Godfrey, Ted Greenwald, Michael Lally, Ann Lauterbach, Gerard Malanga, Alice Notley, John Perreault, Carter Ratcliff, Rene Ricard, Peter Schjeldahl, Tony Towle, Bill Zavatsky.

Robert Miller Gallery, New York. "Alex Katz: Cutouts." February 21–March 17. Exhibition catalogue, essay by Carter Ratcliff.

Benjamin Mangel Gallery, Philadelphia. "Alex Katz: Cutouts." November 15, 1979–January 10, 1980.

Susanne Hilberry Gallery, Birmingham, Michigan. "Alex Katz: Cutouts and Drawings." November 17–December 22.

1980

Hartnell College Gallery, Salinas, California. "Alex Katz: Rush— An Environmental Wall Piece." February 11–March 14. Traveled to University Art Museum, University of California, Santa Barbara, November 12–December 14. Exhibition catalogue, introduction by Gary Smith; essay by David Ligare.

Marlborough Gallery Inc., New York. "Alex Katz." March 1–29. Exhibition catalogue.

The Queens Museum, Flushing, New York. "Alex Katz: Scale and Gesture." March 8–April 27. Exhibition brochure, foreword by Janet Schneider.

Fine Arts Gallery, State University of New York, Stony Brook. "Alex Katz: Ada." April 14–May 10.

Mira Godard Gallery, Toronto. "Alex Katz." April 26–May 21.

Middendorf/Lane Gallery, Washington, D.C. "Alex Katz: Cutouts." November 15–December 11.

Fay Gold Gallery, Atlanta. "Alex Katz: Drawings, Paintings, Sculpture & Prints." November 19–December 31.

Centro Colombo-Americano, Bogotá, Colombia. "Alex Katz." November 26–December 19.

1981

Robert Miller Gallery, New York. "Alex Katz: 1957–59." February 5–March 7. Exhibition catalogue, essay by Irving Sandler.

Portland Center for the Visual Arts, Oregon. "Alex Katz." February 19–March 22.

Susanne Hilberry Gallery, Birmingham, Michigan. "Alex Katz: Paintings." May 5–June 6.

Birmingham Museum of Art, Alabama. "Alex Katz." May 14–June 21. Exhibition brochure, essay by Richard N. Murray.

Contemporary Arts Center, Cincinnati. "Alex Katz: Paintings and Drawings 1959–79." September 17–November 1.

Mira Godard Gallery, Toronto. "Alex Katz: Painted Metal Cutouts." October 17–November 4.

Middendorf/Lane Gallery, Washington, D.C. "Alex Katz: Cutouts." November 15–December 11.

1982

Susanne Hilberry Gallery, Birmingham, Michigan. "Alex Katz: Drawings." January 8–30.

Marlborough Fine Art Ltd., London. "Alex Katz: Recent Paintings." January 13–February 6. Exhibition catalogue, introduction by John Russell.

John C. Stoller and Co., Minneapolis. "Alex Katz: Cut-Outs." January 15–March 15.

Marlborough Gallery Inc., New York. "Alex Katz: Drawings 1944–81." March 3–27. Exhibition catalogue, essay by Sanford Schwartz.

Brooke Alexander Gallery, New York. "Alex Katz: Recent Prints." April 17–May 15.

Mira Godard Gallery, Toronto. "Alex Katz: Drawings." June 5–30.

Hokin Gallery, Chicago. "Alex Katz: Cutouts." June 11–July 31.

1983

Marlborough Gallery Inc., New York. "Alex Katz: Recent Paintings." March 5–April 2. Exhibition catalogue.

Hokin Gallery, Palm Beach, Florida. "Alex Katz: Small Paintings." March 8–26.

Susanne Hilberry Gallery, Birmingham, Michigan. "Alex Katz: Small Paintings." March 19–April 16.

Texas Gallery, Houston. "Alex Katz: Recent Cutouts." March 29–April 23.

Harcus Gallery, Boston. "Alex Katz." April 16–May 17.

1984

Robert Miller Gallery, New York. "Alex Katz: Small Paintings from 1950 to the Present." January 5–28.

Michael H. Lord Gallery, Milwaukee. "Alex Katz: Small Paintings from the 1950s to the Present." April 3–May 1.

Benjamin Mangel Gallery, Philadelphia. "Alex Katz." April 6–30.

Asher/Faure Gallery, Los Angeles. "Alex Katz: Paintings." May 5–June 2.

The Picker Art Gallery, Charles A. Dana Creative Arts Center, Colgate University, Hamilton, New York. "Alex Katz—Process and Development: Small Paintings from the Collection of Paul J. Schupf '58." September 10–November 4. Exhibition catalogue, preface by Dewey F. Mosby; introduction by Paul J. Schupf; essay by Gail Levin.

1985

Houghton Gallery, Cooper Union for the Advancement of Science and Art, New York. "Alex Katz Paints a Picture." February 5–23. Exhibition catalogue, introduction by Rene Ricard.

Robert Miller Gallery, New York. "Alex Katz: An Exhibition of Recent Cutouts." March 5–30.

Marlborough Fine Art Ltd., Tokyo. "Alex Katz." April 13–May 25. Exhibition catalogue, essay by Takahiko Okada.

William A. Farnsworth Library and Art Museum, Rockland, Maine. "Alex Katz." July 11–September 15. Exhibition catalogue, preface by Marius B. Peladeau; introduction by Marilyn Solvay; interview by Vincent Katz.

Colby College Museum of Art, Waterville, Maine, and Bowdoin College Museum of Art, Brunswick, Maine. "Alex Katz: An Exhibition Featuring Works from the Collection of Paul J. Schupf." July 18–October 6. Exhibition catalogue, interview with Alex Katz and Paul J. Schupf by Sylvie Skira.

Mario Diacono Gallery, Boston. "Alex Katz: *Twelve Hours*." November 8–30. Exhibition brochure, essay by Mario Diacono.

Edwin A. Ulrich Museum of Art, Wichita State University, Kansas. "Paintings by Alex Katz." November 13, 1985–January 5, 1986.

GROUP EXHIBITIONS

1951

Peter Cooper Gallery, New York. "Jean Cohen and Alex Katz: Paintings." January 20–February 10.

1953

Tanager Gallery, New York. "Lois Dodd and Alex Katz: Paintings." May 8–30.

1954

Tanager Gallery, New York. "Paintings and Sculpture." December 20, 1954–January 20, 1955.

1955

Stable Gallery, New York. "The New York Artists Annual." May 1–21.

1956

Stable Gallery, New York. "The New York Artists Annual." May 22–June 16.

1957

Tanager Gallery, New York. "Tom Boutis and Alex Katz: Collages." November 23–December 7.

1959

Tanager Gallery, New York. "Metropolitan Younger Artists." October 16–November 5. Exhibition catalogue, foreword by Irving Sandler.

1960

The Pennsylvania Academy of the Fine Arts, Philadelphia. "The One Hundred and Fifty-fifth Annual Exhibition: American Painting and Sculpture." January 24–February 28. Exhibition catalogue, foreword by E. P. Richardson.

Tanager Gallery, New York. "Elaine de Kooning, Jane Freilicher, Alex Katz." February 19–March 11.

Whitney Museum of American Art, New York. "Young America 1960: Thirty American Painters under Thirty-six." September 14–October 30. Traveled to The Baltimore Museum of Art, November 16, 1960–January 1, 1961; Contemporary Arts Center, Cincinnati, January 16–February 22, 1961; City Art Museum of St. Louis, March 8–April 15, 1961; Columbus Gallery of Fine Arts, May 1–June 5, 1961. Exhibition catalogue, foreword by Lloyd Goodrich and John I. H. Baur.

David Herbert Gallery, Los Angeles. "Appearance and Reality." September-October. Exhibition catalogue, essay by James Schuyler.

1961

The Art Institute of Chicago. "64th American Exhibition: Paintings and Sculpture." January 6–February 5. Exhibition catalogue, foreword by John Maxon.

Visual Arts Gallery, School of Visual Arts, New York. "The Figure: Then and Now." November 20–December 15.

1962

Kornblee Gallery, New York. "Figures." May-June. Exhibition catalogue, introduction by Jack Kroll.

1963

The Poses Institute of Fine Arts, Brandeis University, Waltham, Massachusetts. "Recent Acquisitions: The Gevirtz-Mnuchin Collection and Related Gifts." Organized for travel to The Kootz Gallery, New York, March 26–30; Rose Art Museum, Brandeis University, Waltham, Massachusetts, May 3–June 2. Exhibition catalogue, introduction by Sam Hunter.

The Poses Institute of Fine Arts, Brandeis University, Waltham, Massachusetts. "New Directions in American Painting." Organized for travel to Munson-Williams-Proctor Institute Museum of Art, Utica, New York, December 1, 1963–January 5, 1964; Isaac Delgado Museum of Art, New Orleans, February 7–March 8, 1964; Atlanta Art Association, March 18–April 22, 1964; J. B. Speed Art Museum, Louisville, Kentucky, May 4–June 7, 1964; Indiana University Art Museum, Bloomington, June 22–September 20, 1964; Washington University, St. Louis, October 5–30, 1964; The Detroit Institute of Arts, November 10–December 6, 1964. Exhibition catalogue, text by Sam Hunter.

Colby College Museum of Art, Waterville, Maine. "Maine and Its Artists: 1710–1963." Exhibition catalogue, essays by Robert E. L. Strider and Edith K. Jelke.

1964

Wadsworth Atheneum, Hartford. "Contemporary American Figure Painting: Group Show." May 7–31.

Colby College Museum of Art, Waterville, Maine. "Maine: 100 Artists of the 20th Century." June 25–September 30. Exhibition catalogue, introduction by Christopher Huntington; essay by Robert E. L. Strider.

Wilcox Gallery, Swarthmore College, Swarthmore, Pennsylvania. "Two Generations of Modern American Painting." Exhibition catalogue, introduction by Harold Rosenberg.

The Museum of Modern Art, New York. "Recent Landscapes by Eight Americans." Organized for travel in the United States and Europe. Exhibition catalogue, introduction by Frank O'Hara.

1965

Weatherspoon Art Gallery, University of North Carolina, Greensboro. "Art on Paper 1965." November 1–25. Exhibition catalogue, preface by Stark S. Dillard; foreword by Gilbert Carpenter.

The Museum of Modern Art, New York. "American Collages." May 11–July 25. Traveled in the United States and Europe. Exhibition catalogue, introduction by Kynaston McShine.

1966

Museum of Art, Rhode Island School of Design, Providence. "Recent Still Life." February 23–April 4. Exhibition catalogue, introduction by Daniel Robbins.

The Jewish Museum, New York. "Harry N. Abrams Family Collection." June 29–September 5. Exhibition brochure, introduction by Sam Hunter; interview with Harry N. Abrams.

Milwaukee Art Center. "The Inner Circle." September 15–October 23. Exhibition catalogue, essay by Tracy Atkinson.

Museum Boymans-van Beuningen, Rotterdam, The Netherlands. "Amerikaanse Schilderijen Collages." September 20–October 30. Exhibition catalogue, essay by R. Hammacher van den Brande.

Bowdoin College Museum of Art, Brunswick, Maine. "The Walter K. Gutman Collection." October 14–November 27. Exhibition catalogue, foreword by Marvin Sadik; introduction by Walter Gutman.

The Museum of Modern Art, New York. "Two Decades of American Painting." Organized for travel in Japan, India, and Australia. Exhibition catalogue, preface by Waldo Rasmussen; essays by Irving Sandler, Lucy R. Lippard, G. R. Swenson.

1967

Yale University Art Gallery, New Haven. "The Helen W. and Robert M. Benjamin Collection." May 4–June 18. Exhibition catalogue, introduction by Andrew C. Ritchie; text by Lloyd Goodrich.

The Jewish Museum, New York. "Large-Scale American Paintings." July 11–September 10.

Susanne Lemberg Usdan Gallery, Bennington College, Bennington, Vermont. "Recent Figurative Art." October 5–29.

Whitney Museum of American Art, New York. "1967 Annual Exhibition of Contemporary Painting." December 13, 1967–February 4, 1968. Exhibition catalogue.

1968

Vassar College Art Gallery, Poughkeepsie, New York. "Realism Now." May 8–June 12. Exhibition catalogue, introduction by Linda Nochlin.

Galleries of the National Academy of Design, New York. "Skowhegan School of Painting & Sculpture: Annual Art Exhibition & Sale." October 4–13. Exhibition catalogue, foreword by John I. H. Baur.

Weatherspoon Art Gallery, University of North Carolina, Greensboro. "Art on Paper 1968." November 17–December 18. Exhibition catalogue, foreword by John H. Dillard; introduction by Walter Barker.

Finch College Art Gallery, New York. "The Dominant Woman." December 13, 1968–January 26, 1969. Exhibition catalogue, foreword by Elayne H. Varian; text by Walter Gutman.

1969

American Federation of Arts, New York. "Patriotic Images in American Art." Organized for travel to Cedar Rapids Art Center, Iowa, January 19–February 9; Decatur Art Center, Illinois, March 2–23; Greenville County Museum of Art, South Carolina, April 13–May 4.

Philbrook Art Center, Tulsa. "The American Sense of Realism." March 4–25. Concurrently at Museum of Art, University of Oklahoma, Norman, and Oklahoma Art Center, Oklahoma City, April 6–May 11. Exhibition catalogue, preface by Donald G. Humphrey.

Windham College, Putney, Vermont. "The Romantic Landscape in Contemporary Art." April–May. Exhibition catalogue, introduction by Dore Ashton.

Milwaukee Art Center. "Directions 2: Aspects of a New Realism." June 21–August 10. Traveled to Contemporary Arts Museum, Houston, September 17–October 19; Akron Art Institute, November 9–December 14. Exhibition catalogue, essays by Tracy Atkinson and John Lloyd Taylor.

The Museum of Modern Art, New York. "Contemporary Portraits." Organized for travel in the United States. Exhibition brochure, text by Alicia Legg.

The Museum of Modern Art, New York. "Inflated Images." Organized for travel in the United States and Canada. Exhibition brochure, text by Betsy Jones.

1970

Konsthallen, Göteborg, Sweden. "Warmwind: Amerikanska Realister." March 26–April 12. Exhibition catalogue, introduction by Anders Bergh; essays by Lars Hansson, Magnus Hedlund, Anders Bergh, Lars Johansson.

Colby College Art Museum, Waterville, Maine. "Landscape in Maine: 1820–1970." April 4–May 5. Traveled to Bowdoin College Museum of Art, Brunswick, Maine, May 21–June 28; Carnegie Gallery, University of Maine, Orono, July 8–August 30. Exhibition catalogue, foreword and essays by James M. Carpenter, David O. Decker, Hugh J. Gourley, Richard V. West.

Indianapolis Museum of Art. "Painting & Sculpture Today." April. Exhibition catalogue, preface by Carl J. Weinhardt, Jr.; foreword by Robert J. Rohn; introduction by Richard L. Warrum.

The Art Museum, Princeton University, Princeton, New Jersey. "American Art Since 1960." May 6–27. Exhibition catalogue, introduction by Sam Hunter; essays by John Hand, Michael D. Levin, Peter P. Morrin.

Walker Art Center, Minneapolis. "Figures—Environments." May 15–June 13. Traveled to Cincinnati Art Museum, October 2–November 1; Dallas Museum of Fine Arts, December 13, 1970–January 17, 1971. Exhibition catalogue, essays by Dean Swanson and Martin Friedman.

1971

The Corcoran Gallery of Art, Washington, D.C. "Thirty-second Biennial Exhibition of Contemporary American Painting." February 28–April 4. Exhibition catalogue, introduction by Walter Hopps.

American Academy and Institute of Arts and Letters, New York. "An Exhibition of Contemporary Painting and Sculpture." March 4–April 10.

Suffolk Museum, Stony Brook, New York. "The Contemporary Figure and a New Realism." August 14–October 7. Exhibition catalogue, introduction by Jane des Grange; essay by June Blume.

Hudson River Museum, Yonkers, New York. "20th-Century Painting and Sculpture." October 2–November 14. Exhibition catalogue, foreword by Howard Conant; introduction by Irving Sandler.

Weatherspoon Art Gallery, University of North Carolina, Greensboro. "Art on Paper 1971." November 14–December 17. Exhibition catalogue, foreword by John H. Dillard; introduction by James E. Tucker.

Pennsylvania Academy of the Fine Arts, Philadelphia. "Return to the Figure." December 9, 1971–January 9, 1972.

San Francisco Museum of Art. "Color/Constructivism/Realism in Contemporary Graphics." December 28, 1971–February 13, 1972. Exhibition catalogue, essay by Suzanne Foley.

1972

Whitney Museum of American Art, New York. "1972 Annual Exhibition: Contemporary American Painting." January 25–March 19. Exhibition catalogue, foreword by John I. H. Baur.

The Parrish Art Museum, Southampton, New York. "Contemporary American Flower Painting." June 9–July 4.

1973

Whitney Museum of American Art, New York. "1973 Biennial Exhibition: Contemporary American Art." January 10–March 18. Exhibition catalogue, foreword by John I. H. Baur.

The William Benton Museum of Art, University of Connecticut, Storrs. "Selections from the New York University Art Collection." March 12–April 15. Exhibition catalogue, preface by Ruth Bowman; introduction by Stephanie Terenzio.

Whitney Museum of American Art, New York. "American Drawings 1963–73." May 25–July 22. Exhibition catalogue, essay by Elke H. Solomon.

Seattle Art Museum. "American Art: Third Quarter Century." August 22–October 14. Exhibition catalogue, text by Jan van der Marck; foreword by Thomas N. Maytham and Robert B. Dootson.

Yale University Art Gallery, New Haven, Connecticut. "American Drawings 1970–73." October 9–November 25. Exhibition catalogue, introduction by Christina Orr.

The Cleveland Museum of Art. "Contemporary American Artists." December 18, 1973–February 10, 1974. Exhibition catalogue, introduction by Tom Hinson.

1974

Allan Frumkin Gallery, New York. "American Painting in Watershed Year '61." March 9–April 2. Exhibition catalogue, introduction by Allan Frumkin.

Lowe Art Museum, University of Miami, Coral Gables, Florida. "Contemporary Portraits by American Painters." October 3–November 10. Exhibition catalogue, introduction by John Gruen.

Whitney Museum of American Art, Downtown Branch, New York. "New Portraits." November 7–December 12. Exhibition brochure.

The Queens Museum, Flushing, New York. "New Images: Figuration in American Painting." November 16–December 29. Exhibition catalogue, introduction by Peter Tatistcheff and Janet Schneider.

The Brooklyn Museum, New York. "19th National Print Exhibition." November 20, 1974–January 5, 1975. Traveled to Fine Arts Gallery of San Diego, February 15–March 30, 1975. Exhibition catalogue, introduction by Jo Miller.

1975

Louis K. Meisel Gallery, New York. "Watercolors and Drawings: American Realists." January 1–31. Exhibition catalogue, introduction by Susan Pear Meisel.

Allan Frumkin Gallery, New York. "Portrait Painting 1970–75: A Survey of Informal Portraiture in the USA." January 7–31. Exhibition catalogue, essays by G. W. Barrette and Allan Frumkin.

University Art Museum, University of New Mexico, Albuquerque. "Lithography I: First Biennial Exhibition of Contemporary Lithography." March 2–April 13. Exhibition catalogue, foreword by Cleta Downy; introduction by Clinton Adams.

New Jersey State Museum, Trenton. "Modern Views of George Washington." September 5–October 27.

De Cordova and Dana Museum and Park, Lincoln, Massachusetts. "Candid Painting: American Genre 1950–75." October 12–December 7. Exhibition catalogue, text by Eva Jacob.

Museum of Fine Arts of St. Petersburg, Florida. "Figure as Form: American Painting 1930–75." November 25, 1975–January 4, 1976. Traveled to Florida Center for the Arts, University of South Florida, Tampa, January 12–February 6, 1976; Columbus Museum of Arts and Crafts, Columbus, Georgia, March 8–April 14, 1976. Exhibition catalogue, introduction by Bradley Nickels; essay by Margaret A. Miller.

1976

Westminster College Art Gallery, New Wilmington, Pennsylvania. "In Praise of Space: Part II—Recent American Landscape Art." January 6–February 26. Traveled to Parson School of Design Galleries, New York, April 1976; Gross-McCleaf Galleries, Philadelphia, August 2–31. Exhibition catalogue, introduction by Robert Godfrey; essays by Robert Godfrey, Bonnie Sklavski, Michael Eisenman, Barbara White.

The Corcoran Art Gallery, Washington, D.C. "America 1976: A Bicentennial Exhibition Sponsored by the U.S. Department of the Interior." April 27–June 6. Traveled to the Wadsworth Atheneum, Hartford, July 4–September 12; Fogg Art Museum, Harvard University, Cambridge, Massachusetts, October 19–December 7, simultaneously at the Institute of Contemporary Art, Boston; The Minneapolis Institute of Arts, January 16–February 27, 1977; Milwaukee Art Center, March 19–May 15, 1977; Fort Worth Art Museum, June 18–August 14, 1977; San Francisco Museum of Art, September 10–November 13, 1977; The High Museum of Art, Atlanta, December 10, 1977–February 5, 1978; The Brooklyn Museum, New York, March 11–May 21, 1978. Exhibition catalogue, foreword by Thomas S. Kleppe; essays by Robert Rosenblum, Neil Welliver, John Ashbery, Richard Howard.

Institute of Contemporary Art, Boston. "A Selection of American Art: The Skowhegan School 1946–76." June 16–September 5. Traveled to Colby Museum of Art, Colby College, Waterville, Maine, October 1–30. Exhibition catalogue, preface by Gabriella Jeppson; introduction by Lloyd Goodrich; essays by Bernarda B. Shahn and Allen Ellenzweig.

The Grey Art Gallery and Study Center, New York University. "Inaugural Exhibition: New York University Grey Art Gallery and Study Center." September 22–October 16. Exhibition catalogue, foreword by Kenneth L. Mathis; introduction by Joy L. Gordon, essay by Abby Weed Grey.

Weatherspoon Art Gallery, University of North Carolina, Greensboro. "Art on Paper 1976." November 14–December 15. Exhibition catalogue, introduction by Gilbert F. Carpentek.

The Brooklyn Museum, New York. "30 Years of American Printmaking." November 20, 1976–January 30, 1977. Exhibition catalogue, foreword by Michael Botwinick; essay by Gene Baro.

1977

Museum of Art, Washington State University, Pullman. "Works on Paper: American Art 1945–75." February 28–April 1. Exhibition catalogue, essay by Rosalind Krauss.

Everson Museum of Art, Syracuse, New York. "Provincetown Painters: 1890s–1970s." April 1–June 26. Traveled to Provincetown Art Association, August 15–September 5. Exhibition catalogue, foreword by Ronald A. Kuchta; text by Dorothy Gees Seckler.

Vancouver Art Gallery, British Columbia, Canada. "Studies and Other Initial Works." May 7–June 7. Exhibition catalogue, introduction by Christopher Varley.

New York State Museum, Albany. "New York: The State of Art." October 8–November 27. Exhibition catalogue, foreword by Governor Hugh L. Carey; essays by Robert Bishop, William H. Gerdts, Thomas B. Hess.

Thorpe Intermedia Gallery, Sparkill, New York. "Outside the City Limits: Landscape by New York Artists." October 16–November 13. Exhibition catalogue, preface by Roger Howrigan and Adele Myers; introduction by Lola B. Gellman; essays by John Perreault and Carter Ratcliff.

Philadelphia College of Art. "Artists' Sets and Costumes." October 31–December 17. Exhibition catalogue, introduction by Janet Kardon.

1978

Sarah Lawrence College Art Gallery, Bronxville, New York. "Artists' Sets and Costumes: Recent Collaborations Between Painters and Sculptors and Dance, Opera and Theatre." January 24–February 19.

Whitney Museum of American Art, New York. "20th Century American Drawings: Five Years of Acquisitions." July 28–October 1. Exhibition catalogue, introduction by Tom Armstrong; essay by Paul Cummings.

The High Museum of Art, Atlanta. "Children in America: A Study of Images and Attitudes." September 30, 1978–May 27, 1979. Exhibition catalogue, foreword by Paula Hancock; introduction by Charles Strickland; essay by Rosamond Olmsted Humm.

The Sydney and Frances Lewis Foundation Collection, Richmond. "Late Twentieth-Century Art." Organized for travel in the United States. Exhibition catalogue, introduction by Frederick R. Brandt and Susan L. Butler.

1979

Whitney Museum of American Art, New York. "1979 Biennial Exhibition." February 6–April 8. Exhibition catalogue, preface by Tom Armstrong; foreword by John G. Hanhardt, Barbara Haskell, Richard Marshall, Mark Segal, Patterson Sims.

Fine Arts Gallery, University of Colorado, Boulder. "Six Painters of the Figure." March 5–April 7. Exhibition catalogue, essay by Jean-Edith Weiffenbach.

Ralph Wilson Gallery, Lehigh University, Bethlehem, Pennsylvania. "24th Annual Contemporary American Painting Exhibition: The Revival of Realism." March 9–April 19. Exhibition catalogue, introduction by Bunin Askin.

Centro Colombo-Americano, Bogotá, Colombia. "16 Realists of New York." March 22–April 26. Exhibition catalogue, essay by Jaime Maique Ardila and Gonzalo Ariza.

Whitney Museum of American Art, New York. "The Decade in Review: Selections from the 1970s." June 19–September 2. Exhibition brochure, essay by Patterson Sims.

Heckscher Museum, Huntington, New York. "As We See Ourselves: Artists' Self-Portraits." June 22–August 5. Exhibition catalogue, foreword and essay by Katherine Lochridge.

Aspen Center for the Visual Arts, Colorado. "American Portraits of the Sixties + Seventies." June-August. Exhibition catalogue, essay by Julie Auger; introduction by Philip Yenawine.

The Metropolitan Museum of Art, New York. "Recent Acquisitions from the Department of Twentieth-Century Art." October 16, 1979–January 30, 1980.

The Denver Art Museum. "Poets & Painters." November 21, 1979–January 13, 1980. Exhibition catalogue, foreword by Dianne Perry Vanderlip; essay by David Shapiro.

Dorothy Rosenthal Gallery, Chicago. "Four Realist Artists Selected by Jack Beal and Alex Katz." December 1, 1979–January 16, 1980.

1980

The Hickory Museum of Art, Hickory, North Carolina. "Woman: Images on Paper." January 6–27. Traveled to Sheraton Square Gallery, Charlotte, North Carolina, March 5–April 13; Fayetteville Museum of Art, Fayetteville, North Carolina, June 8–29; Asheville Art Museum, Asheville, North Carolina, August 12–September 21; St. John's Museum of Art, Wilmington, North Carolina, October 16–November 22; Wilkes Art Gallery, North Wilkesboro, North Carolina, August 1–31, 1982.

Munson-Williams-Proctor Institute Museum of Art, Utica, New York. "The Olympics in Art: An Exhibition of Works Related to Olympic Sports." January 13–March 2. Exhibition catalogue, foreword by Joseph S. Trovato; essays by D. R. Edward Wright, Bartlett H. Hayes, Jr., Gary Hoenig.

The Museum of Modern Art, New York. "Printed Art: A View of Two Decades." February 14–April 1. Exhibition catalogue, preface and essay by Riva Castleman.

Montgomery Museum of Fine Arts, Alabama. "American Painting of the Sixties & Seventies: The Real/The Ideal/The Fantastic: Selections from the Whitney Museum of American Art." April 4–May 25. Traveled to Joslyn Art Museum, Omaha, July 25–September 14; Museum of Fine Arts of St. Petersburg, Florida, September 28–November 9; Columbus Museum of Art, Ohio, December 8, 1980–January 15, 1981; Colorado Springs Fine Arts Center, February 1–March 21, 1981; Sierra Nevada Museum of Art, Reno, April 11–May 23, 1981. Exhibition catalogue, preface by Tom Armstrong; foreword by Philip A. Klopfenstein.

Danforth Museum, Framingham, Massachusetts. "Aspects of the 70's: Directions in Realism." May 17–August 24. Exhibition catalogue, foreword by Joy L. Gordon; essay by John Perreault.

Naussau County Museum of Fine Art, Roslyn Harbor, New York. "Contemporary Naturalism: Works of the 1970s." June 8–August 24. Exhibition catalogue, preface by Phyllis Stigliano; introduction by Lawrence Alloway.

Whitney Museum of American Art, New York. "The Figurative Tradition and the Whitney Museum of American Art: Paintings and Sculpture from the Permanent Collection." June 25–September 28. Exhibition catalogue, foreword by Tom Armstrong; essays by Patricia Hills and Roberta K. Tarbell.

McIntosh-Drysdale Gallery, Washington, D.C. "An American Collection." September-October. Traveled to University of Virginia Art Museum, Charlottesville, October 19–November 19. Exhibition catalogue, preface by Michael Rea; introduction by Jane Livingston.

The Edmonton Art Gallery, Edmonton, Alberta, Canada. "2nd Canadian Biennale of Prints and Drawings." September 5–October 19. Exhibition catalogue, preface by Walter Jule; essay by Maggie Callahan.

Cranbrook Academy of Art Museum, Bloomfield Hills, Michigan. "The Changing Canvas." September 14–October 26. Exhibition catalogue, introduction by John J. Hohmann; text by Julie Hall.

Philbrook Art Center, Tulsa. "Realism/Photorealism." October 5–November 23. Exhibition catalogue, foreword by Jesse G. Wright, Jr.; essay by John Arthur.

The Chrysler Museum, Norfolk, Virginia. "American Figure Painting 1950–80." October 17–November 30. Exhibition catalogue, text by Thomas W. Styron.

The Brooklyn Museum, New York. "American Drawing in Black & White: 1970–80." November 22, 1980–January 18, 1981. Exhibition brochure, essay by Gene Baro.

1981

The Maryland Institute College of Art, Baltimore. "The Human Form: Interpretations." February 8–March 2. Exhibition brochure, introduction by Fred Lazarus IV.

Miami University Art Museum, Oxford, Ohio. "A Seventies Selection: An Exhibition of Works from the Permanent Collection of the Whitney Museum of American Art." February 14–June 14. Exhibition catalogue, introduction by David Berreth.

San Antonio Museum of Art. "Real, Really Real, Super Real." March 1–April 26. Traveled to Indianapolis Museum of Art, May 19–June 28; Tucson Museum of Art, July 19–August 26; Museum of Art, Carnegie Institute, Pittsburgh, October 24–January 3, 1982. Exhibition catalogue, introduction by Sally Boothe-Meredith; essays by Alvin Martin, Linda Nochlin, Philip Pearlstein; interviews by Sally Boothe-Meredith and Alvin Martin.

The Museum of Modern Art, New York. "Recent Drawing Acquisitions." March 19–June 2.

Hirschl & Adler Modern, New York. "The Contemporary American Landscape." May 2–29. Exhibition catalogue, essay by Frank H. Goodyear, Jr.

Provincetown Art Association and Museum, Massachusetts. "The Sun Gallery." July 24–August 30. Exhibition catalogue, preface by Annabelle Herbert; poem by Dominic Falcone; essay by Irving Sandler.

Akron Art Museum. "The Image in American Painting & Sculpture: 1950–80." September 12–November 8. Exhibition catalogue, preface by Michael Danoff; introduction by Carolyn Kinder Carr.

Pennsylvania Academy of the Fine Arts, Philadelphia. "Contemporary American Realism Since 1960." September 18–December 13. Traveled to Virginia Museum of Fine Arts, Richmond, February 1–March 28, 1982; The Oakland Museum, May 6–July 25, 1982; Gulbenkian Foundation, Lisbon, Portugal, September 29–October 27, 1982; Salas y Exposiciones, Madrid, Spain, November 17, 1982–January 8, 1983; Kunsthalle, Nuremberg, West Germany, February 11–April 10, 1983. Exhibition catalogue, text by Frank H. Goodyear, Jr.

Whitney Museum of American Art, Fairfield County, Stamford, Connecticut. "The American Landscape: Recent Developments." October 23–December 9. Exhibition brochure.

Pratt Manhattan Center Gallery, Pratt Institute, New York. "Sculpture in the 70s: The Figure." November 3–25. Traveled to Arizona State University, Tempe, October 25–November 29; Dartmouth College Museum, Hanover, New Hampshire, January 14–March 15, 1982. Exhibition catalogue, introduction by Ellen Schwartz.

Museo Rufino Tamayo, Mexico City. "Arte Contemporaneo Internacional." Exhibition catalogue, introduction by Manuel Reyero.

1982

Zabriskie Gallery, New York. "Flat and Figurative 20th-Century Wall Sculpture." January 6–February 6.

Fraunces Tavern Museum, New York. "Twentieth-Century Images of George Washington." February 1–April 30. Exhibition brochure, essay by Robert I. Goler.

Museum of Fine Arts, Boston. "A Private Vision: Contemporary Art from the Graham Gund Collection." February 9–April 4. Exhibition catalogue, essays by Carl Belz, Kathy Halbreich, Kenworth Moffett, Elisabeth Sussman, Diane W. Upright.

National Museum of American Art, Washington, D.C. "Recent Trends in Collecting: Twentieth-Century Painting and Sculpture from the National Museum of American Art." February 12–March 28. Exhibition catalogue, statement by Henry Lowe; essays by Joshua C. Taylor and Harry Rand; comments by Merry Foresta, Lynda Roscoe Hartigan, Sara Hutchinson, Virginia M. Mecklenburg.

Munson-Williams-Proctor Institute Museum of Art, Utica, New York. "An Appreciation of Realism." February 13–April 1. Exhibition catalogue, text by John Manning.

Contemporary Arts Center, New Orleans. "The Human Figure." March 6–April 10. Exhibition catalogue, essay by Alexandra Monett.

Whitney Museum of American Art, Fairfield County, Stamford, Connecticut. "Five Artists and the Figure." April 9–June 9. Exhibition brochure.

Whitney Museum of American Art, New York. "Focus on the Figure: Twenty Years." April 15–June 13. Exhibition brochure, essay by Barbara Haskell.

The Aldrich Museum of Contemporary Art, Ridgefield, Connecticut. "Homo Sapiens: The Many Images." May 9–September 5. Exhibition catalogue, introduction by Martin Sosnoff.

Weatherspoon Art Gallery, University of North Carolina, Greensboro. "20th-Century Figural Images on Paper." Organized for travel to Tulane University, New Orleans, September 6–October 4; Gertrude Herbert Memorial Institute of Art, Augusta, Georgia, January 10–February 7, 1983; Columbus College Art Gallery, Columbus, Georgia, September 12–October 9, 1983; University of Tennessee, Knoxville, January 7–February 4, 1984; University of North Carolina, Charlotte, February 10–March 11, 1984. Exhibition catalogue, foreword by James E. Tucker.

Museum of Fine Arts, Boston. "Contemporary Realists Painting." November 3, 1982–February 27, 1983.

Pennsylvania Academy of the Fine Arts, Philadelphia. "Perspectives on Contemporary American Realism: Works of Art on Paper from the Collection of Jalane and Richard Davidson." December 17, 1982–February 20, 1983. Traveled to The Art

Institute of Chicago, April 1–May 20, 1983. Exhibition catalogue, preface by Richard J. Boyle; text by Frank H. Goodyear, Jr.

1983

The Chrysler Museum, Norfolk, Virginia. "The Sailor 1930–45: The Image of an American Demigod." January 20–March 13. Exhibition catalogue, essay by Thomas W. Sokolowski.

Center Gallery, Bucknell University, Lewisburg, Pennsylvania. "Faces Since the 50s: A Generation of American Portraiture." March 11–April 17. Exhibition catalogue.

Galerie Zabriskie, Paris. "Quatre Américains." July 6–September 10.

The Parrish Art Museum, Southampton, New York. "The Painterly Figure." July 24–September 14. Exhibition catalogue, foreword by Trudy C. Kramer; essay by Klaus Kertess.

Linda Farris Gallery, Seattle. "Self-Portraits." August 5–September 11. Exhibition catalogue, introduction by Linda Farris; essay by Peter Frank.

The Brooklyn Museum, New York. "The American Artist as Printmaker." October 28, 1983–January 22, 1984. Exhibition catalogue, text by Barry Walker.

1984

Marlborough Fine Art Ltd., Tokyo. "International Masters of Contemporary Figuration." February 20–April 7. Exhibition catalogue.

American Academy and Institute of Arts and Letters, New York. "Paintings and Sculpture by Candidates for Art Awards." March 5–April 1.

Whitney Museum of American Art, New York. "American Art Since 1970: Painting, Sculpture, and Drawings from the Collection of the Whitney Museum of American Art, New York." Organized for travel to La Jolla Museum of Contemporary Art, California, March 10–April 22; North Carolina Museum of Art, Raleigh, September 29–November 25; Sheldon Memorial Art Gallery, University of Nebraska, Lincoln, January 12–March 3, 1985; Center for the Fine Arts, Miami, March 30–May 26, 1985. Exhibition catalogue, essay by Richard Marshall.

Hillwood Art Gallery, C. W. Post Center, Greenvale, New York. "Artist in the Theatre." March 16–April 12. Traveled to Guild Hall Museum, East Hampton, New York, June 9–July 15. Exhibition catalogue, preface by Judy K. van Wagner and Helen A. Harrison; essays by Susan Davis and Robert Dash.

The Parrish Art Museum, Southampton, New York. "Painting Naturally: Fairfield Porter and His Influences." April 15–June 3. Exhibition catalogue, essay by Prescott Schutz.

SELECTED BIBLIOGRAPHY

STATEMENTS, INTERVIEWS, AND BOOKS BY THE ARTIST

Statement in "Is There a New Academy? Part II." *Art News*, 58 (September 1959), p. 39.

Ashbery, John, and Alex Katz. *Fragment*. Los Angeles: Black Sparrow Press, 1966.

Statement in Barbara Rose and Irving Sandler, "The Sensibility of the Sixties." *Art in America*, 55 (January-February 1967), p. 50.

Statement in "Jackson Pollock: An Artists' Symposium, Part I." *Art News*, 66 (April 1967), p. 32.

Koch, Kenneth, and Alex Katz. *Interlocking Lives*. New York: Kulchur Press, 1970.

Statement in Gerrit Henry, "The Artist and the Face: A Modern American Sampling." *Art in America*, 63 (January-February 1975), p. 36.

Interview by Carter Ratcliff in "New York Today: Some Artists Comment." *Art in America*, 65 (September-October 1977), pp. 81-82.

Mathews, Harry, and Alex Katz. *Selected Declarations of Dependence*. Calais, Vermont: Z Press, 1977.

Statement in "Talk on Signs and Symbols." Edited by Kenward Elmslie. *ZZZZZZ*. Calais, Vermont: Z Press, 1977.

Interview by Jacqueline Brody in "New Prints of Worth: A Question of Taste." *Print Collector's Newsletter*, 10 (September-October 1979), pp. 109-119.

Interview by Kate Horsfield in "On Art and Artists: Alex Katz." *Profile*, 2 (January 1982), pp. 1-11.

Interview by Ada Katz in "Alex Katz." *Profile*, 2 (January 1982), pp. 12-21.

Statement in Mark Strand, ed. *Art of the Real: Nine American Figurative Painters*. New York: Clarkson N. Potter, 1983.

Interview by Vincent Katz in "Plunk 'em Down and Paint 'em." *The Ritz Newspaper*, no. 92 (1984), p. 59.

Ratcliff, Carter, and Alex Katz. *Give Me Tomorrow*. New York: Vehicle Editions, 1985.

MONOGRAPHS AND CATALOGUES

Field, Richard S. *Alex Katz* (exhibition catalogue). Middletown, Connecticut: Davison Art Center, Wesleyan University, 1974.

————, and Elke M. Solomon. *Alex Katz Prints* (exhibition catalogue). New York: Whitney Museum of American Art, 1974.

Levin, Gail. *Alex Katz—Process and Development: Small Paintings from the Collection of Paul J. Schupf '58* (exhibition catalogue). Preface by Dewey F. Mosby; introduction by Paul J. Schupf. Hamilton, New York: The Picker Art Gallery, Charles A. Dana Creative Arts Center, Colgate University, 1984.

Ligare, David. *Alex Katz: Rush—An Environmental Wall Piece* (exhibition catalogue). Salinas, California: Hartnell College Gallery, 1980.

Maravell, Nicholas P. *Alex Katz: The Complete Prints.* Interview by Carter Ratcliff. New York: Alpine Fine Arts Collection, 1983.

Ratcliff, Carter. *Alex Katz* (exhibition catalogue). New York: Marlborough Gallery Inc., 1973.

————. *Alex Katz: Cutouts* (exhibition catalogue). New York: Robert Miller Gallery, 1979.

Ricard, Rene. *Alex Katz Paints a Picture* (exhibition catalogue). New York: Houghton Gallery, Cooper Union for the Advancement of Science and Art, 1985.

Rosenblum, Robert. *Alex Katz: Recent Paintings* (exhibition catalogue). Fresno, California: Fresno Arts Center and Museum, 1977.

Russell, John. *Alex Katz: Recent Paintings* (exhibition catalogue). London: Marlborough Fine Art Ltd., 1982.

Sandler, Irving. *Alex Katz.* New York: Harry N. Abrams, 1979.

————. *Alex Katz* (exhibition catalogue). New York: Tanager Gallery, 1959.

————. *Alex Katz: 1957–1959* (exhibition catalogue). New York: Robert Miller Gallery, 1981.

————, and William Berkson, eds. *Alex Katz.* Essays by Lucy Lippard, Robert Rosenblum, David Antin, Ron Padgett. New York: Frederick A. Praeger, 1971.

Schwartz, Sanford. *Alex Katz: Drawings 1944–1981* (exhibition catalogue). New York: Marlborough Gallery Inc., 1982.

Smith, Roberta. *Alex Katz in the Seventies* (exhibition catalogue). Waltham, Massachusetts: Rose Art Museum, Brandeis University, 1978.

ARTICLES AND REVIEWS

Alloway, Lawrence. "Alex Katz's Development." *Artforum*, 14 (January 1976), pp. 45–51.

————. "Art." *The Nation*, December 6, 1971, pp. 605–6.

————. "Art." *The Nation*, October 1, 1977, pp. 316–17.

————. "The Constant Muse." *Art in America*, 69 (January 1981), pp. 110–18.

Antin, David. "Alex Katz and the Tactics of Representation." *Art News*, 70 (April 1971), pp. 44–47, 75–77.

Berkson, William. "Alex Katz's Surprise Image." *Arts Magazine*, 40 (December 1965), pp. 22–26.

Bourdon, David. "Katz Advertises His Family." *The Village Voice*, March 15, 1976, pp. 131–32.

B[urton], S[cott]. "Reviews and Previews: Alex Katz." *Art News*, 67 (October 1968), p. 12.

Calas, Nicolas. "Alex Katz: Faces and Flowers." *Art International*, 11 (November 20, 1967), pp. 25–27.

Denby, Edwin. "Katz: Collage, Cutout, Cut-up." *Art News*, 63 (January 1965), pp. 42–44.

Disch, Thomas M. "The Katz Chronicle." *The Village Voice*, September 28, 1982, pp. 67–70.

G[eist], S[idney]. "Galleries: '52–'53 Flashback." *Arts Digest*, 27 (June 1953), pp. 21, 24.

G[oodnough], R[obert]. "Reviews and Previews: Alex Katz, Lois Dodd." *Art News*, 52 (May 1953), pp. 55–56.

Hess, Thomas B. "Alex Katz's Sign of the Times." *New York*, October 3, 1977, pp. 68–70.

Kent, Sarah. "Alex Katz at the Marlborough Gallery." *Studio International*, 189 (March-April 1975), pp. 149–50.

Kramer, Hilton. "Art: Zoom Lens Canvases of Alex Katz." *The New York Times*, March 3, 1978, section C, p. 18.

————. "Art View: Two Illuminating Styles of the Late 1950's." *The New York Times*, February 15, 1981, section D, pp. 29, 31.

————. "Fortnight in Review: Alex Katz." *Arts Digest*, 29 (November 1954), p. 29.

————. "Quite a Lot to Look At." *The New York Times*, November 28, 1971, section D, p. 21.

————. "The Return of the Realists—And a New Battle Shaping Up." *The New York Times*, October 25, 1981, section C, pp. 1, 35.

————. "The Sociable Art of Alex Katz." *The New York Times*, December 24, 1967, section 2, p. 24.

————. "The World of Alex Katz: Big Numbers, Fast Moves." *The New York Times*, December 16, 1973, section D, p. 25.

K[roll], J[ack]. "Quartet of March Solos: Katz." *Art News*, 60 (March 1961), pp. 38, 67.

————. "Reviews and Previews: Alex Katz." *Art News*, 61 (February 1963), p. 11.

Leider, Phillip. "Reviews: Alex Katz." *Artforum*, 6 (February 1968), pp. 46–47.

McGill, Douglas C. "How Alex Katz Puts Power on Canvas." *The New York Times*, March 24, 1985, section 2, pp. 1, 33.

Moritz, Charles, ed. "Alex Katz." *Current Biography*, 36 (July 1975), pp. 17–20.

Muchnich, Suzanne. "Alex Katz Paints the Good Life." *Artweek*, September 17, 1977.

O'Hara, Frank. "Alex Katz." *Art and Literature*, no. 9 (Summer 1966), pp. 91–101. Reprinted in Frank O'Hara. *Art Chronicles 1954–1966.* New York: George Braziller, 1975.

————. "Art Chronicle II." *Kulchur* (Summer 1962).

————. "Reviews and Previews: Alex Katz." *Art News*, 53 (November 1954), p. 66.

erreault, John. "At the Table, On the Stoop." *The Village Voice*, December 20, 1973, pp. 37, 39.

————. "Cool Katz." *SoHo Weekly News*, March 19, 1980, p. 50.

errone, Jeff. "Reviews: Alex Katz." *Artforum*, 16 (May 1978), pp. 58–59.

[orter], F[airfield]. "Reviews and Previews: Young Painters." *Art News*, 53 (November 1954), pp. 53, 59.

————. "Art." *The Nation* (April 2, 1960), p. 243.

————. "Art." *The Nation* (October 1, 1960), pp. 215–16.

atcliff, Carter. "Alex Katz: Style as a Social Contract." *Art International*, 22 (February 19, 1978), pp. 26–28, 50–51.

————. "Alex Katz's Cutouts." *Arts Magazine*, 53 (February 1979), pp. 96–97.

————. "The New York Letter." *Art International*, 15 (December 20, 1971), pp. 60–61.

ussell, John. "Art: Alex Katz's Idyllic and Simplified World." *The New York Times*, February 28, 1976, p. 22.

————. "Art: Alex Katz's Works, Ever Nice, Never Empty." *The New York Times*, March 11, 1983, section C, p. 22.

————. "Art People." *The New York Times*, September 7, 1979, section C, p. 14.

————. "Art View: When a Pastime Becomes the Stuff of Metaphor." *The New York Times*, March 17, 1985, section 2, p. 31.

————. "Katz Portraits Step Out of Their Frames." *The New York Times*, March 2, 1979, section C, pp. 1, 17.

andler, Irving. "Alex Katz at Marlborough." *Art in America*, 62 (March-April 1974), pp. 110–11.

————. "Alex Katz 1957–1959." *Arts Magazine*, 55 (February 1981), pp. 98–99.

————. "In the Art Galleries." *The New York Post*, February 9, 1964, p. 40.

————. "The New Cool Art." *Art in America*, 52 (February 1965), pp. 96–100.

[awin], M[artica]. "In the Galleries: Alex Katz." *Arts Magazine*, 31 (January 1957), pp. 53, 56.

————. "In the Galleries: Tom Boutis and Alex Katz." *Arts Magazine*, 32 (January 1958), p. 58.

Schuyler, James. "Alex Katz Paints a Picture." *Art News*, 60 (February 1962), pp. 38–41, 52.

————. "Reviews and Previews: Alex Katz." *Art News*, 53 (January 1959), p. 15.

Schwartz, Ellen. "Alex Katz: 'I See Something and Go Wow.'" *Art News*, 78 (Summer 1979), pp. 42–46.

————. "Alex Katz Paints a Picture." *Art News*, 78 (Summer 1979), pp. 46–47.

Schwartz, Sanford. "Alex Katz So Far." *Art International*, 17 (December 15, 1973), pp. 28–30, 58.

Silverthorne, Jeanne. "Reviews: Alex Katz." *Artforum*, 18 (Summer 1980), p. 80.

Smith, Roberta. "Art: Expression without the Ism." *The Village Voice*, March 29, 1983, p. 81.

————. "Art: Surface Effects." *The Village Voice*, January 31, 1984, pp. 82–83.

————. "Reviews: Alex Katz." *Artforum*, 12 (March 1974), p. 74.

Steinbrink, Mark. "Why Artists Design for Paul Taylor." *The New York Times*, April 3, 1983, section 2, pp. 1, 24.

Sterns, Robert. "Alex Katz: Paintings and Drawings 1959–1979." *Ohio Arts Journal*, September-October 1981.

Tallmer, Jerry. "Portraits Far Larger Than Life." *The New York Post*, March 11, 1978, p. 16.

Tillim, Sidney. "The Katz Cocktail: Grand and Cozy." *Art News*, 64 (December 1965), pp. 46–49, 67–69.

————. "Month in Review." *Arts Magazine*, 35 (April 1961), pp. 46–49.

T[yler], P[arker]. "Reviews and Previews: Alex Katz." *Art News*, 55 (January 1957), p. 55.

Wallach, Amei. "In Katz' Art, Only Happy Endings." *Newsday*, March 16, 1980, section II, pp. 4–5.

WORKS IN THE EXHIBITION

Dimensions are in inches, followed by centimeters; height precedes width.

PAINTINGS

Four Children, 1951–52
Oil on board, 18 × 18 (45.7 × 45.7)
Collection of Jean Cohen

Winter Scene, 1951–52
Oil on board, 24 × 24 (61 × 61)
Collection of the artist

After Softball, 1953
Oil on board, 24 × 24 (61 × 61)
Collection of the artist

Two Figures, 1954
Oil on board, 32 × 32 (81.3 × 81.3)
Collection of the artist

Two Trees, 1955
Oil on board, 32 × 32 (81.3 × 81.3)
Robert Miller Gallery, New York

Ives Field, 1956
Oil on board, 32 × 32 (81.3 × 81.3)
Robert Miller Gallery, New York

Track Jacket, 1956
Oil on board, 24 × 18 (61 × 45.7)
Collection of the artist

Ada in Black Sweater, 1957
Oil on board, 24 × 18 (61 × 45.7)
Robert Miller Gallery, New York

Self-Portrait (Cigarette), 1957
Oil on board, 36 × 24 (91.4 × 61)
Robert Miller Gallery, New York

Ada in White Dress, 1958
Oil on canvas, 60 × 48 (152.4 × 121.9)
Collection of Mr. and Mrs. Jack N. Greenman

Eli at Ducktrap, 1958
Oil on canvas, 49 × 71 (124.5 × 180.3)
Private collection

Irving and Lucy, 1958
Oil on canvas, 60 × 60 (152.4 × 152.4)
Collection of Irving and Lucy Sandler

Ada in Blue Housecoat, 1959
Oil on canvas, 80 × 50 (203.2 × 127)
The Rivendell Collection

Bather, 1959
Oil on canvas, 48 × 72 (121.9 × 182.9)
Collection of the artist

Norman Bluhm, 1959
Oil on canvas, 48 × 48 (121.9 × 121.9)
Collection of Paul Jacques Schupf

Double Portrait of Robert Rauschenberg, 1959
Oil on canvas, 66 × 85½ (167.6 × 217.2)
Collection of Paul Jacques Schupf

Paul Taylor, 1959
Oil on canvas, 72 × 84 (182.9 × 213.4)
Collection of the artist

The Black Dress, 1960
Oil on canvas, 72 × 84 (182.9 × 213.4)
Collection of the artist

Luna Park, 1960
Oil on canvas, 40 × 30 (101.6 × 76.2)
Collection of the artist

October # 2, 1962
Oil on canvas, 59 × 49 (149.9 × 124.5)
Robert Miller Gallery, New York

View, 1962
Oil on canvas, 30 × 40 (76.2 × 101.6)
Collection of Rudolph Burckhardt

Passing, 1962–63
Oil on canvas, 72¾ × 79⅝ (182.2 × 202.2)
The Museum of Modern Art, New York; Gift of the Louis and Bessie Adler Foundation Inc., Seymour M. Klein, President

Eli, 1963
Oil on canvas, 72 × 86 (182.9 × 218.4)
Whitney Museum of American Art, New York; Gift of Mr. and Mrs. Herbert Fischbach 64.37

The Red Smile, 1963
Oil on canvas, 78¾ × 114¾ (200 × 292.1)
Whitney Museum of American Art, New York; Purchase, with funds from the Painting and Sculpture Committee 83.3

Paul Taylor, 1964
Oil on canvas, 60 × 60 (152.4 × 152.4)
Collection of Charles and Stephanie Reinhart

Ada with Bathing Cap, 1965
Oil on canvas, 60 × 72 (152.4 × 182.9)
Collection of Paul Jacques Schupf

The Cocktail Party, 1965
Oil on canvas, 72 × 96 (182.9 × 243.8)
Collection of Paul Jacques Schupf

Upside Down Ada, 1965
Oil on canvas, 52 × 63 (132.1 × 160)
Collection of the artist

White Lilies, 1966
Oil on canvas, 93 × 79½ (236.2 × 201.9)
Milwaukee Art Museum; Gift of Jane Bradley Pettit

Ada and Vincent, 1967
Oil on canvas, 95 × 72 (241.3 × 182.9)
Collection of the artist

Ada with Superb Lily, 1967
Oil on canvas, 46½ × 52 (118.1 × 132.1)
The Herbert W. Plimpton Collection on extended loan to the Rose Art Museum, Brandeis University, Waltham, Massachusetts

Impala, 1968
Oil on canvas, 72 × 109 (182.9 × 276.9)
The Cleveland Museum of Art; Purchase Mr. and Mrs. William H. Marlatt Fund and Gift of The Eppler Family Foundation and Agnes Gund Saalfield

Swamp Maple, 4:30, 1968
Oil on canvas, 144 × 93 (365.8 × 236.2)
Collection of the artist

Self-Portrait with Sunglasses, 1969
Oil on canvas, 96 × 68 (243.8 × 172.7)
Virginia Museum of Fine Arts, Richmond; Gift of Sydney and Frances Lewis

Vincent and Tony, 1969
Oil on canvas, 72½ × 120⅞ (184.2 × 307)
The Art Institute of Chicago; Gift of The Society for Contemporary Art

Walk, 1970
Oil on canvas, 72 × 144 (182.9 × 365.8)
Collection of the artist

Sunny, 1971
Oil on canvas, 96¼ × 72¼ (244.5 × 183.5)
Milwaukee Art Museum; Gift of Mrs. Harry Lynde Bradley

Ada and Vincent in the Car, 1972
Oil on canvas, 72 × 96 (182.9 × 243.8)
Hirshhorn Museum and Sculpture Garden, Smithsonian Institution, Washington, D.C.

The Black Jacket, 1972
Oil on canvas, 78 × 144 (198.1 × 365.8)
Collection of Paul Jacques Schupf

Blue Umbrella # 2, 1972
Oil on canvas, 96 × 144 (243.8 × 365.8)
Collection of Paul Jacques Schupf

Swimmer # 3, 1973
Oil on canvas, 60 × 72 (152.4 × 182.9)
Collection of Paul Jacques Schupf

Canoe, 1974
Oil on canvas, 72 × 144 (182.9 × 365.8)
Atlantic Richfield Corporate Art Collection, Los Angeles

Good Afternoon # 2, 1974
Oil on canvas, 72 × 96 (182.9 × 243.8)
Collection of Paul Jacques Schupf

Thursday Night # 2, 1974
Oil on canvas, 72 × 144 (182.9 × 365.8)
Collection of Paul Jacques Schupf

Vincent with Radio, 1974
Oil on canvas, 76 × 96 (193 × 243.8)
Collection of Susan Merians

Moose Horn State Park, 1975
Oil on canvas, 78 × 144 (198.1 × 365.8)
Marlborough Gallery Inc., New York

Roof Garden, 1975
Oil on canvas, 72 × 96 (182.9 × 243.8)
Collection of Paul Jacques Schupf

Twilight, 1975
Oil on canvas, 126 × 96 (320 × 243.8)
Marlborough Gallery Inc., New York

Islesboro Ferryslip, 1976
Oil on canvas, 78 × 84 (198.1 × 213.4)
Collection of Paul Jacques Schupf

Night, 1976
Oil on canvas, 72 × 96 (182.9 × 243.8)
Pennsylvania Academy of the Fine Arts, Philadelphia; Contemporary Arts Purchase Fund

Place, 1977
Oil on canvas, 108 × 144 (274.3 × 365.8)
Whitney Museum of American Art, New York; Gift of Sydney and Frances Lewis 78.23

Round Hill, 1977
Oil on canvas, 72 × 96 (182.9 × 243.8)
Private collection

December, 1979
Oil on canvas, 132 × 108 (335.3 × 274.3)
Marlborough Gallery Inc., New York

His Behind the Back Pass, 1979
Oil on canvas, 72 × 96 (182.9 × 243.8)
Marlborough Gallery Inc., New York

Ada and Alex, 1980
Oil on canvas, 60 × 72 (152.4 × 182.9)
Collection of Alan P. Safir

Red Coat, 1982
Oil on canvas, 96 × 48 (243.8 × 121.9)
Collection of Leslie and Stanley Westreich

The Yellow House, 1982
Oil on canvas, 78 × 72 (198.1 × 182.9)
Marlborough Gallery Inc., New York

Pas de Deux, 1983
Oil on canvas, five panels, 132 × 360 (335.3 × 914.4) overall
Collection of Paul Jacques Schupf

Eleuthera, 1984
Oil on canvas, four panels, 120 × 264 (304.8 × 670.6) overall
Marlborough Gallery Inc., New York

CUTOUTS

Ada Ada, 1959
Oil on wood cutout, 39 × 22 (99.1 × 55.9)
Collection of the artist

Blackie Walking, 1959
Oil on board cutouts, four figures,
10¾ × 16¼ (27.3 × 41.3) overall
Hirshl & Adler Modern, New York

Frank O'Hara, 1959–60
Oil on wood cutout, 60 × 15 (152.4 × 38.1)
Collection of Elaine de Kooning

Portrait of Joe, 1961
Oil on wood cutout, 45¾ × 16⅜ (116.2 × 41.6)
Everhart Museum, Scranton, Pennsylvania

Ada Four Times, 1968
Oil on aluminum cutout, 50½ × 33 (128.3 × 83.8)
Collection of Dr. and Mrs. Terry Podolsky

Alex, 1968
Oil on aluminum cutout, 71 × 18½ (180.3 × 47)
Collection of the artist

One Flight Up, 1968
Oil on aluminum cutouts,
67¾ × 180 × 47 (172.1 × 457.2 × 119.4) overall
Robert Miller Gallery, New York

Rudy and Edwin, 1968
Oil on aluminum cutout, 48 × 43½ (121.9 × 110.5)
Collection of the artist

Ada with Nose, 1969–70
Oil on aluminum cutout, 71½ × 72 (181.6 × 182.9)
Collection of the artist

Sanford Schwartz, 1978
Oil on aluminum cutout, 71 × 10 (180.3 × 25.4)
Collection of Dr. and Mrs. Marvin H. Rivkin

Rudy, 1979
Oil on aluminum cutout, 72 × 10 (182.9 × 25.4)
Collection of the artist

Ada (Black and White Dress), 1980
Oil on aluminum cutout, 69¼ × 4 (175.9 × 10.2)
Mira Godard Gallery, Toronto

Ada, 1982
Oil on aluminum cutout, 36 × 4 (91.4 × 10.2)
Collection of the artist

John, 1982
Oil on aluminum cutout, 36 × 4 (91.4 × 10.2)
Robert Miller Gallery, New York

Marcia, 1982
Oil on aluminum cutout, 36 × 4 (91.4 × 10.2)
Robert Miller Gallery, New York

Bathers (Vincent and Anastasia), 1984
Oil on aluminum cutout, 68 × 45 (172.7 × 114.3)
Robert Miller Gallery, New York

Sunset (Christopher and Kate), 1984
Oil on aluminum cutout, 69½ × 47½ (176.5 × 120.7)
Robert Miller Gallery, New York

COLLAGES

Man with Dog, 1955
Collage, 4 × 6 (10.2 × 15.2)
Collection of Roy Leaf

Olives, 1955
Collage, 8½ × 11 (21.6 × 27.9)
Robert Miller Gallery, New York

Two Figures, 1955
Collage, 4 × 6 (10.2 × 15.2)
Collection of the artist

Roadmaster, 1955–56
Collage, 4½ × 7 (11.4 × 17.8)
Collection of the artist

Pink Beach, 1956
Collage, 5 × 7 (12.7 × 17.8)
Collection of Sanford Schwartz

Raft, 1956
Collage, 5 × 8 (12.7 × 20.3)
Robert Miller Gallery, New York

Two Figures at Lincolnville Beach, 1956–57
Collage, 5 × 8 (12.7 × 20.3)
Collection of the artist

Sunset Cove, 1957
Collage, 4 × 6 (10.2 × 15.2)
Collection of Jane Freilicher and Joseph Hazan

Three People, 1957
Collage, 4 × 6 (10.2 × 15.2)
Robert Miller Gallery, New York

Ada in the Water, 1958
Collage, 5 × 8 (12.7 × 20.3)
Collection of Alice and Leo Yamin

Bathers, 1959
Collage, 4 × 6 (10.2 × 15.2)
Collection of Mr. and Mrs. Fayez Sarofim

Beach House, 1959
Collage, 5 × 7 (12.7 × 17.8)
Collection of the artist

Blueberry Field # 1, 1959
Collage, 14 × 17 (35.6 × 43.2)
Collection of the artist

Sleeping Figure, 1959
Collage, 4¼ × 6½ (10.8 × 16.5)
Collection of Mr. and Mrs. Fayez Sarofim

Dog at End of Pier, 1960
Collage, 8½ × 11¼ (21.6 × 28.6)
Collection of Peter R. Stern

Greenwood Lake, New Jersey, 1960
Collage, 13¼ × 15⅝ (33.7 × 39.7)
International Council of The Museum of Modern Art,
New York

Twilight, 1960
Collage, 13⅞ × 15⅝ (35.2 × 39.7)
International Council of The Museum of Modern Art,
New York

Provincetown, 1971
Collage, 18 × 24 (45.7 × 61)
Robert Miller Gallery, New York

This book was published on the occasion of the exhibition "Alex Katz" at the Whitney Museum of American Art, New York, March 13 – June 15, 1986. It was organized at the Whitney Museum by Doris Palca, Head, Publications and Sales; Sheila Schwartz, Editor; Elaine Koss, Managing Editor; and Emily Russell Sussek, Secretary/Assistant.

PHOTOGRAPH CREDITS

Book design and layout
Daniel Skira and Richard Marshall

Printing and color reproduction
IRL Imprimeries Réunies Lausanne s.a.

Binding
Ateliers Roger Veihl, Geneva

March 1986

Printed in Switzerland